KW-224-230

GOOD HOUSEKEEPING

SALADS

GOOD HOUSEKEEPING

SALADS

GOOD HOUSEKEEPING INSTITUTE

EBURY PRESS LONDON

Published by Ebury Press
National Magazine House
72 Broadwick Street
London W1V 2BP

First impression 1983

© The National Magazine Company 1983

The expression GOOD HOUSEKEEPING as used in the title of this
book is the trade mark of The National Magazine Company Limited
and The Hearst Corporation, registered in the United Kingdom and
the USA, and other principal countries in the world, and is the
absolute property of The National Magazine Company Limited and
The Hearst Corporation. The use of this trade mark other than
with the express permission of The National Magazine Company Limited
or The Hearst Corporation is strictly prohibited.

All rights reserved. No part of this publication may be reproduced,
stored in a retrieval system, or transmitted, in any form or by
any means, electronic, mechanical, photocopying, recording or
otherwise, without prior permission of the publishers.

ISBN 0 85223 262 4

Designed by Roland Blunk
Illustrations by Deborah Bruton

Colour photography by Christine Hanscomb, facing
pages 32, 33, 48, 65, 80, 81, and by Anthony Blake,
facing pages 49, 64.
The publishers would like to thank Harrods Ltd for
its help in providing china and glass for photography.

Jacket photograph by Paul Williams shows Endive,
orange and walnut salad (page 88) Tuna pasta hors
d'oeuvre (page 25) Tossed Italian salad (page 85)
Seafood salad bowl (page 51) and Dressed avocado
(page 30).

Filmset by Advanced Filmsetters (Glasgow) Ltd
Printed and bound in Italy by
New Interlitho S.p.A. Milan

CONTENTS

WHAT MAKES A
GOOD SALAD?

A good salad, be it a starter, side salad or main course, should be fresh, appetising and delicious! It should combine foods with a variety of different flavours and textures and be finished off with a carefully chosen dressing and garnish that make the salad impossible to resist.

Most of us probably still think of a salad as a boring mixture of raw, usually green, foods served as part of a meal, especially in summer. Salads need no longer be boring. The choice of foods that can be used is endless and ingredients can range from the usual lettuce, cucumber and tomato to exotic fruits and vegetables such as avocados and artichokes, and cold cooked foods such as rice, pasta and meats. The recipes in this book combine the ordinary with the extraordinary to make delicious salad dishes, many of which form a meal in themselves as they contain cooked meats, fish, cheese, eggs or dried pulses.

The nutritive value of a salad obviously varies according to its ingredients, but there is no doubt that salads are good for you. Fresh fruits and vegetables, especially valuable when eaten raw, contain high proportions of vitamin C. Extra goodness can be added with a few chopped nuts or some grated cheese.

No salad is complete without a dressing and a garnish. The dressing should be chosen carefully to ensure flavours match and the dressing is not too strong. Garnishes add colour and appeal and can look impressive and difficult to achieve. They are in fact simple and make use of other fresh fruits or vegetables, or of nuts, seeds, olives or herbs, to provide a contrast of colour and flavour that complements the salad perfectly.

VEGETABLES AND OTHER
SALAD PLANTS

To enjoy vegetables and salad plants at their very best, they should be prepared and served as fresh as possible. If you do not grow your own vegetables, select the most fresh-looking produce from your greengrocer or market stall. They should be crisp and free from wilted or discolored leaves or bruises.

Always handle salad foods with care, being careful not to bruise them. The more they are handled, the less goodness they retain. Trim off and discard any damaged or discolored leaves, wash them quickly but thoroughly, and shake them free of any surplus moisture in a tea towel, salad basket or spinner. A little moisture helps keep salad plants crisp but too much hastens deterioration. If you do not intend using them immediately, they will keep for a day or two in the salad drawer of the refrigerator, or loosely wrapped in a polythene bag or cling film at the bottom of the refrigerator.

Leave washed salad foods uncut in the refrigerator until chilled and crisp and required for use, then shred them coarsely with a sharp knife or tear them apart with your hands. It is better not to shred them finely as this causes a greater vitamin loss. (Exceptions to this are iceberg lettuce and Chinese cabbage, which can be sliced.)

GLOBE ARTICHOKE A globe artichoke looks like a large thistle head. It is available all the year round but is still a luxury vegetable with a price to match. Choose those with small, bright green leaves and firm stems. Eating an artichoke is quite an art: you pull off each leaf with your fingers, dip the leaf in melted butter, hollandaise sauce or vinaigrette dressing and suck off the soft base part of the leaf. Hidden under the leaves is the inedible hairy choke which can be removed before serving. Below this is the titbit—the succulent heart or fond. If you're feeling very extravagant, serve only the artichoke hearts.

JERUSALEM ARTICHOKE Jerusalem artichoke is not a true artichoke. It looks nothing like a globe artichoke and has no claim on Jerusalem! It is a twisted, knobbly, brown tuber and its misshapen appearance can be off-putting. However, it has a delicate flavour well worth investigating. Jerusalem artichoke does not store well as it goes soft.

To prepare, scrub well in cold water and trim off any discolored parts. Peeling is more easily done after cooking. Steam, boil or poach for 15–20 minutes. Drain, cool and slice. It is particularly good with a herb French dressing.

ASPARAGUS To prepare asparagus, rinse each stalk very gently to wash away any dirt. Using a sharp knife, scrape or shave the length of each stalk, starting just below the tip. Cut off the bottom end if it is very tough and woody. Trim the stalks to roughly the same length. Place the stalks in a bowl of cold water while preparing the remainder. Tie asparagus into neat bundles of six to eight stalks of an even thickness, heads uppermost. Secure each bundle under the tips and near the base.

Cook asparagus with care. Use a special asparagus pan or wedge the bundles upright in a deep saucepan. The pan should contain enough boiling salted water to come three quarters of the way up the stalks. Cover the tips with a cap made of foil and simmer gently for about 10 minutes, until tender. This ensures the stalks are poached while the delicate tips are gently steamed. Drain carefully and leave to cool.

AUBERGINE Also known as eggplant, melanzana and garden egg, the aubergine is a member of the potato family, even though it doesn't look like its relation. It comes in different sizes but is easily recognised by its oval shape and plush, shiny, purple skin.

The juice of the aubergine is slightly bitter, so after removing the stalk (but not the skin) cut it into 0.5-cm ($\frac{1}{4}$-inch) slices and sprinkle them with salt to draw out the juice. Leave for 30 minutes before washing off, then dry well with absorbent kitchen paper. Aubergines can be fried, baked or simmered then chilled to serve as a salad. They're also delicious halved and stuffed.

AVOCADO Unless you want a ripe avocado to eat that day, buy firm fruit and let them ripen at home at room temperature for 1–3 days or more slowly in the refrigerator for up to a week. The avocado is ripe when it yields to gentle pressure. Remove from the refrigerator several hours before serving.

Just before serving, slice the avocado in half lengthways, making a cut that completely encircles the avocado and penetrates to the stone. Gently rotate the halves in opposite directions until they separate, and ease out the stone. If wished, peel and slice. Brush or toss in lemon juice to prevent discoloration.

BEANS, broad If the pods are only 5–7.5 cm (2–3 inches) long and the beans hardly formed, they can be cooked and eaten whole in the pod. However, if they are large, which is usually the case, they should be podded, cooked and then slipped out of their outer skins after cooking, serving only the tender green beans inside. Both are suitable for salads. Cook in boiling salted water for 15–20 minutes. Drain, plunge straight into cold water and drain again.

BEANS, French Young French beans, or haricot verts, are slender and stringless. They are delicious served cold in a salad. For a simple salad, top and tail, then cook the beans lightly in boiling salted water for about 10 minutes. Drain well and then plunge into cold water and drain again—this helps to retain their bright green colour and will also keep them crisp. Turn the cooked beans into a serving dish, pour over French dressing and chill well. Serve sprinkled with chopped herbs.

Frozen haricot verts can also be used in salads. Cook in boiling salted water for about 10 minutes then drain, plunge into cold water and drain again before adding to a salad.

BEAN SPROUTS Bean sprouts are now a popular purchase in super-markets and greengrocers. They can also be grown at home in a jam jar or on a tray or plate from seeds. Added raw to a salad they provide a crisp texture, a delicate flavour and are very nutritious. The seeds can be bought in packets from wholefood shops and include mung beans, alfalfa, fenugreek and alphotoco sprouts.

The mung bean is most commonly used for growing bean sprouts. Soak 225–450 g (8 oz–1 lb) beans overnight in a warm place and they will begin to sprout. Transfer them either into a large screw-topped jar or on to a tray covered with absorbent paper (kitchen paper or blotting paper) in a polythene bag. Keep in a warm dark place for 5–6 days until the bean sprouts are 5–7 cm (2–3 inches) tall. Every day rinse bean sprouts in a jar with clean cold water, or 'water' bean sprouts on a tray.

They must be kept constantly moist and warm—in the dark for white shoots and in the light for green ones.

To prepare bean sprouts for a salad, simply rinse them under running cold water and drain well. Any stray roots and hulls need not be removed as they are full of vitamins and flavour.

BEETROOT Beetroot is a popular salad ingredient. To prepare, cut off the stalks 2.5 cm (1 inch) or so above the root, then wash the beetroots, taking care not to damage the skin or they will 'bleed' when boiled. Boil in salted water until soft. The time depends on the age and freshness: small early beetroots will take about 30 minutes, larger older ones about $1\frac{1}{2}$ hours.

When the beetroots are cooked, thinly peel off the skin. Cut into thin slices if the beetroots are small; grate or dice them if large. The prepared beetroot can be sprinkled with salt, pepper and a very little sugar and covered with vinegar or a mixture of vinegar and water. This helps it to keep and also gives it a better flavour. Raw beetroot can be grated and added to salads in small quantities.

Canned beetroot can also be used in salads. Drain off the can liquor and add the beetroot to the salad.

BROCCOLI Broccoli makes an excellent salad if blanched, chilled and served with mayonnaise or French dressing. Cut broccoli stalks into slices and the heads into florets. Cook in boiling salted water for 5 minutes. Drain, plunge into ice-cold water and drain again.

CALABRESE Calabrese is a green sprouting variety of broccoli with numerous shoots. It should be cooked like asparagus, with the heads above the water so they don't get damaged, in a tall pan of boiling salted water for 10 minutes. It's nice served cold with mayonnaise or French dressing.

BRUSSELS SPROUTS Left uncooked, early season Brussels sprouts make an interesting salad when shredded and tossed in a French dressing.

CABBAGE
GREEN CABBAGES The two varieties of green cabbage that are suitable for salads are summer and winter cabbages. Avoid the strong, dark green varieties.

SUMMER CABBAGES are in season from June onwards. This sweeter cabbage can be cut into wedges or coarsely shredded and used in salads.

WINTER CABBAGES are in season from September to December. They are coarser in texture and stronger in flavour than summer cabbages but are also suitable for using in salads.

RED CABBAGES are in season from November to March. They can be served raw in salads.

WHITE CABBAGES are in season from October to February. They should be very pale in colour, round and heavy for their size. They are usually finely shredded and used in coleslaw-type salads.

CHINESE CABBAGE, OR CHINESE LEAVES, looks like a large Cos lettuce but has a mild cabbage taste. The oval heart is tightly encased in almost white leaves It is very crisp, so is ideal for salads. It is also very economical and, unlike ordinary lettuce, it will keep for two weeks in the refrigerator. Trim away the root end and any damaged outer leaves, shred it with a knife as the leaves are too big to leave whole, then wash.

CARROT Carrots make a super salad ingredient—simply grate them raw and add to salads to give colour and flavour. Blanched slices or cubes of carrot make a refreshing salad when tossed in French dressing, soured cream or yoghurt and sprinkled with chopped fresh herbs.

CAULIFLOWER This may be added to salads cooked or uncooked. In either case, break it into florets—small ones if to be used raw. When buying or choosing a cauliflower for salads, look for fresh green leaves surrounding a white firm 'curd' with no blemishes or bruises.

CELERIAC Celeriac is an odd-looking vegetable, like a misshapen warty turnip, but it has a pronounced celery flavour. It should feel heavy for its size—if light it's probably hollow and spongy. It can be eaten raw or cooked. Scrub it thoroughly and cut off all the fibres and roots (some may be fairly deep). It will need peeling thickly. If you're eating it raw, slice or grate it and serve with French dressing or mayonnaise. To cook, slice and boil in salted water for 10–15 minutes.

CELERY Celery can be added to most salads for extra crunch and flavour, or used as a garnish in the form of celery curls (see page 22). Separate the sticks, trim off the ends and wash the sticks well in cold water, scrubbing to remove any dirt from the grooves. Slice or chop.

CHICORY There has always been confusion over the name of chicory, the spear-shaped vegetable with tightly packed fresh leaves. The French and Americans call it endive and call endive (the curly leaved lettuce—see page 11) chicory!

Chicory is grown in darkness to produce crisp white leaves. A greeny tinge at the tip of the leaves usually means that the chicory will be bitter. Do not use very bitter chicory for salads.

As a salad ingredient, chicory may be sliced or quartered or the separated leaves may be served whole. To prepare, trim off the root and any damaged leaves, then wash, if necessary, although chicory is usually remarkably clean. Do not leave the heads soaking in cold water as this tends to increase the bitterness.

COURGETTE Courgettes or Zucchini, as they are called in Italy and America, are from the squash/marrow family. Although usually grown as a separate plant, courgettes can in fact be the baby fruits cut from marrow plants before fully developed, while the yellow flower head is still attached.

Tender young courgettes can be served in a salad. Slice and cook in boiling salted water for 2–3 minutes, then drain, plunge into cold water and drain again. Serve cold with French dressing. They should never be peeled as most of the flavour is in the skin.

CUCUMBER Cucumbers are usually eaten raw, sliced, in salads. Wipe the skin and either leave it on or peel it off thinly. (To crimp a cucumber see page 22.) Slice the cucumber finely, sprinkle with salt and leave it for about 1 hour. Pour off the liquid and rinse. Alternatively, you can soak the cucumber in a little vinegar, with salt and a pinch of sugar. If you like the cucumber crisp use it when freshly sliced.

DANDELION Both the wild dandelion, picked while still young and tender, and cultivated plants make a tasty peppery salad. The leaves can be eaten raw but are best blanched in boiling water for 2–3 minutes then drained and plunged into cold water and drained again. Dandelion is particularly good combined with bacon and tossed in a French dressing.

ENDIVE Dark at the top and paler inside, this is a very pretty salad vegetable. During the winter, frilly endive is a crisp alternative to lettuce and doesn't wilt so quickly. Don't use the outside 'fronds'; choose the paler green ones. Trim off the root end, remove the coarse outer leaves, separate the remaining leaves, wash and drain well.

FENNEL Fennel, usually called Florence fennel, is sold in shops here, but is pricey because it needs a warm climate and two years' growth. It has a distinct aniseed flavour which is very refreshing when used in salads. The whole of fennel is edible. The bulbous stem is good served raw in salads, and the feathery leaves make a pretty garnish. Trim off the top stems and slice off the base before slicing or grating the fennel.

GARLIC Usually only one or two cloves of garlic are needed for the average bowl of salad to provide a subtle garlic flavour. The flavour of garlic can change an ordinary salad into something quite special. First remove the papery outside of the clove, then crush the clove with a little salt using a broad-bladed knife. (Do this on a plate unless you have a board that you keep specially for onion chopping.) Alternatively, use a garlic press, if you have one. Scrape the crushed garlic into the salad bowl or add it to the dressing.

If a crushed clove of garlic is too strong to include in a salad, rub it in a crust of bread, or a slice of French bread, and place the bread in the salad bowl. This crust is then tossed with the salad ingredients and dressing just before serving, then pushed to the bottom of the bowl out of sight. In France, this crust is called a *chapan* and is not really intended to be eaten, though it is considered a great delicacy by enthusiastic garlic eaters! Alternatively, simply rub the sides of the salad bowl with a cut clove of garlic before putting in the salad.

KOHLRABI Kohlrabi is related to cabbage but looks more like a turnip with leaves growing all over the bulb rather than out of the top. There are several varieties distinguished by their skin colour—purple, white or green. It's best when young, so buy kohlrabi around 5 cm (2 inches) in diameter, and eat quickly as it doesn't store well. Trim the base, cut off the leaves and stalks, then peel. Slice thinly or grate and serve with mayonnaise or French dressing.

LEEK Crisp, tender young leeks make an excellent salad if blanched and tossed in a French dressing. Trim and slice the leeks thinly and wash very thoroughly. Blanch in boiling salted water for 3–4 minutes. Drain, plunge immediately into cold water, then drain again.

LETTUCE Lettuce is probably the most familiar salad ingredient but there are several varieties to choose from. Webb's Wonder and Great Lakes are the large, compact, solid variety of lettuce which stay beautifully crisp. The Iceberg lettuce is a particularly crisp, crunchy, solid, round lettuce and its great advantage is that it tastes good, looks good and keeps for weeks without wilting. Although it often seems expensive, the solid weight and keeping qualities make it as economical as the cheaper round lettuce. Other varieties to choose from include the delicious-tasting summer-long lettuce, the baby Cos known as Little Gem or Sugar Cos; while for looks and crispness, there is Sugar Bowl with endive-like, curled leaves.

Cos lettuces have long, crisp green leaves, pale green hearts and a sweet taste. The round or cabbage lettuce has softer, easily bruised leaves. These are available all the year round, while the tastier varieties dominate the summer months. A red lettuce can also occasionally be found—the Radiccio which comes from Italy.

Lettuce has always been considered good for the digestion as it stimulates the gastric juices. Because it also has a cleansing or refreshing effect on the palate, it has become customary in France to eat a lettuce and parsley salad after the fish and meat courses.

To prepare lettuce, trim off the base and discard any outer damaged or wilted leaves. Separate the remaining leaves and cut the heart into wedges, if necessary. Wash quickly but thoroughly in cold water, drain and shake off any excess moisture. Dry in a tea towel or salad basket or in a lettuce 'spin dryer'. Shred coarsely with a sharp knife or tear into pieces with your hands. If a lettuce is a little wilted after washing, place it in a polythene bag and crisp it up in the bottom of the refrigerator for about 30 minutes before use.

LAMBS LETTUCE This is a type of lettuce, also called corn salad and *mâche*. It is available during the winter months and used extensively for salads in France, but is not so readily available here. There are several varieties, both round leaf and long leaf, all tasting much the same. It has succulent, firm, fleshy-textured leaves.

MANGE TOUT Mange tout are under-developed peas specially grown so the pods have no parchment lining. The whole thing is edible, hence its name. They are also known as snow peas, Chinese peas or sugar peas. Top and tail and remove any side strings before boiling for 2 minutes in salted water or steaming for 5 minutes. Drain, plunge into cold water and drain again before using in a salad. If they are very young they can be eaten raw.

MUSHROOMS Button mushrooms are particularly attractive in salads. Trim the base of the stalks, wipe and thoroughly dry, if necessary. Halve or slice thinly and use in salads. Try to avoid peeling mushrooms as most of their goodness is in the skin.

MUSTARD AND CRESS These tiny-leafed ingredients often get lost in a tossed salad and are therefore best used in little bunches as a garnish. Snip them out of the punnet, trimming off the roots and lower parts of the stems with scissors. Place the leaves in a colander or sieve and wash them (under a fast-running cold tap if possible), turning the cress over and removing any seeds.

ONION There are four main varieties: pickling (or button) onions, shallots, common British maincrop and Spanish onions. All can be served in a salad, either braised and chilled or sliced and fried until golden and crispy and sprinkled on top of a salad. Spanish onions are much larger than ordinary onions and have a milder, sweeter flavour. They may be eaten raw in salads. Silverskin onions are white fleshed, silvery skinned and very small; and because of their size and mild sweet flavour they're a popular pickling variety. They can be used straight from the jar, tossed in a salad or used as a garnish.

SPRING ONIONS Spring onions are often served raw in salads. Trim off the root end and remove the papery outer skin. Trim the green leaves down to about 5 cm (2 inches) and wash. They may be sliced and mixed into a salad or a dressing, or they can be used as a garnish (see page 22).

PARSNIP Very young parsnips can be used in salads and make an interesting addition to winter salads. They should be blanched first. To prepare, trim and peel thinly, then cut into cubes or leave whole. Place in a pan of cold salted water, bring to the boil, cook for 2–3 minutes, then drain. Plunge into cold water and drain again.

PEAS After podding, cook peas in boiling salted water for 10–15 minutes until just tender, then drain, plunge into cold water and drain again before adding to a salad. Fresh petit pois may be eaten raw or lightly cooked. Frozen peas should be cooked (follow the instructions on the packet), then blanched and cooled as for fresh peas, before adding to a salad.

PEPPERS Peppers are usually picked when green. They turn yellowy-orange and finally red when fully matured. There is little difference between red and green peppers, although the red ones are a little sweeter and softer. A new variety of white and purple peppers that are grown in Holland are also available here. Peppers will store well for about a week in the refrigerator. Wash, cut off the top to remove the stalk, then cut in half lengthways to remove the seeds and membrane from inside. Slice thinly to use in salads. Cut peppers should be wrapped or kept in a polythene container.

RADISHES Radishes are a popular salad ingredient and also make a colourful garnish (see page 22). There are many varieties and apart from the familiar pink and red varieties there are white and yellow ones. Trim off the root end and leaves and wash the radishes in cold water. Leave whole or slice thinly for a salad.

The Spanish grow a variety of radishes which has a thick black skin and is round and turnip-shaped, or long like a stumpy carrot. These are hardy and grow to a large size without spoiling. They need to be peeled and the inner white flesh can be eaten raw.

SALSIFY Salsify is a long, thin root vegetable. It looks a bit like a parsnip but tastes more like a turnip. Some people find the flavour reminiscent of oysters—hence its other names, oyster plant and oyster vegetable. Peel salsify and cut it into pieces before cooking. If not cooking immediately, place the slices in a bowl of water with a little lemon juice added to prevent discoloration. Cook salsify pieces in boiling salted water, with a little lemon juice added, for 25–30 minutes until tender but still crisp. Salsify can be eaten raw in a salad if chopped or grated finely.

SEAKALE Seakale looks like a cross between rhubarb and celery. The stalks are white and topped with dry, green leaves. Seakale is forced in greenhouses, so it is available in the winter, and grown outside for the spring. The stalks have a nutty flavour and should be very crisp. Don't buy any which are wilting or discolored. It can be eaten raw in a salad, or cooked in boiling salted water, with a little lemon juice added, for 4–5 minutes, then drained, cooled and used in a salad.

SEAKALE BEET Seakale beet, also known as Swiss chard, silver beet or white beet, is a member of the beetroot family. It is grown mainly for its leaves which look very much like spinach leaves but have coarser, crisper centre ribs which are used as a separate vegetable. Seakale beet is hardier than summer spinach and can be bought from autumn until spring.

The leaves of seakale beet can be cooked in exactly the same way as spinach leaves, tearing them from their centre ribs which can be eaten like seakale—hence the name.

SORREL Sorrel is both a wild and cultivated plant with a strong acid flavour. The leaves are best for salads when young and tender. Prepare and use in the same way as spinach. It is good with a French dressing and crispy bacon pieces.

SPINACH Delicately-flavoured summer spinach is light green in colour with tender leaves and stalks, while winter spinach and perpetual spinach (grown and harvested all the year round) are much darker green in colour. It has coarser-textured leaves and stalks and a much stronger flavour. The tender summer variety makes an excellent (raw) salad. Wash thoroughly, then shred, discarding any tough stalks.

SWEETCORN Corn cut from the cob can be added to salads. Fresh cobs should first be trimmed and leaves and silk removed. To remove corn from the cob, hold the cob upright on a work surface and, with a sharp knife, cut away the corn with a downward movement. Work around the lower half of the cob and, when all the corn has been removed, turn the cob the other way up and repeat. Do not try to remove all the corn in one downward cut.

Cook corn off the cob in a little boiling water for 5–10 minutes. Salt should not be added to the water as it toughens the kernels. Drain well, cool and stir into a salad. Frozen and canned sweetcorn can also be used in salads. Canned sweetcorn needs no cooking and can be drained and added straight from the can. Frozen sweetcorn should be cooked in boiling water according to packet instructions and then drained and plunged into cold water and drained again before it is added to a salad.

TOMATOES Tomatoes are a delicious fresh salad ingredient and there are now many varieties available in all shapes and sizes with skins coloured from green to deep red. These include the most commonly available Guernsey and home-grown tomatoes, the very large continental or beef tomatoes and the very small cherry tomatoes.

Remove the stems and wash or wipe the tomatoes. To skin them, dip in boiling water for about 30 seconds, then in cold water and peel off the skins. Alternatively, hold each tomato on a fork over a low gas flame until the skin is blistered all over. The skin can then easily be peeled away.

TURNIP Sweet, tender, early turnips have a slightly mustard flavour and may be eaten raw in moderation. They have green and white skins and are sold in bunches from April until July. Peel thickly and grate these turnips into salads. Maincrop turnips, available for the rest of the year, are not suitable for salads.

WATERCRESS Watercress is a popular salad ingredient with a distinct peppery taste. It is eaten raw in a salad and looks very attractive when mixed with contrasting paler green lettuce or endive leaves. It is also often used as a garnish. Trim the coarse ends from the stalks, wash the watercress and drain well before using.

HERBS WITH SALADS

There are few rules about which herb goes best with which food. They may be varied to suit individual taste and availability. Fresh herbs are always preferable to dried and should be used whenever possible.

Parsley can be added to almost any salad. There are two varieties—curly parsley and flat-leaf continental parsley. Mint and chives are also very popular for serving with salads. Others, which are not always so easy to obtain, are tarragon, which is excellent with poultry and mushrooms; oregano; the less pungent marjoram, which goes well with seafood or is delicious with cold pork sausages. It also goes well with tomatoes, but the ideal herb for a tomato salad is basil, served the Italian way in an olive oil and wine vinegar dressing. Basil is also good in potato salad and coleslaw. Other classic partnerships are dill and cucumber; summer savory and green beans; rosemary and lamb, poultry or seafood. Sage and thyme may also be used on salads, but sparingly.

FRUITS IN SALADS

A wide variety of fruits can be used to give salads an additional, and sometimes more unusual, combination of flavours and textures. A hint of sweetness adds extra interest to a salad and the colour of fruit can make a salad all the more appealing.

APPLE Both cooking and eating apples can be used in salads to add juicy crispness. After peeling, if preferred, core and chop, slice or grate the apples and toss them in lemon juice to prevent discoloration. The bright green, crisp varieties, eg Granny Smith, make particularly good salad apples, as do any with a red skin to add colour.

APRICOT Fresh or canned apricots can be used. Fresh apricots should be halved and stoned before adding to the salad. Canned apricot halves need only to be drained and sliced, if liked.

BANANA After peeling, slice and toss bananas in lemon juice to prevent discoloration. A salad with bananas in will not keep well; if possible, peel, slice and add bananas just before serving.

CHINESE GOOSEBERRY Also known as Kiwi fruit, Carambole or Caromandel, this fruit is egg-shaped with brown hairy skin. The fruit has a soft, juicy green flesh, pitted with black seeds. It tastes a little like a water melon with a hint of strawberry and has the richest vitamin C content of any fruit. The fruit is ready to eat when soft. Peeled, sliced and dipped in lemon juice, they make a very attractive garnish for salads.

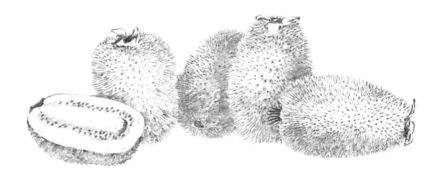

GRAPEFRUIT When using grapefruit in a salad, try to remove as much of the peel and white pith as possible. When segmenting a grapefruit, use a sharp serrated knife to cut the fruit segments out from between the membrane and discard as much of the membrane as possible. Alternatively, grapefruit can be cut into thin slices after peeling and removing the pith. While preparing the fruit, hold it over a bowl to catch any juice that can be used to make the salad dressing.

GRAPES Both green and black grapes are suitable for salads. They should be washed, halved and seeded, if wished, before use.

MANGO Mango is a large stone fruit varying in size from the size of a peach to up to 2.5 kg ($5\frac{1}{2}$ lb). Some are round, others heart- or kidney-shaped. The tough skins range in colour from green to yellow or orange. They are delicious served chilled—the flavour is something like a cross between an apricot and a pineapple. Peel, stone and slice them to add to salads.

MELON All varieties of melon can be used in salads. Their different flavours and colours make an interesting addition. Halve melons and scoop out and discard the seeds. Either scoop the fruit out in balls with a Parisian cutter, or cut the melon into wedges and cut the fruit away from the skin with a sharp knife. Cube, slice or chop the fruit as required.

ORANGE These should be prepared and segmented or sliced in the same way as grapefruit.

PAWPAW Pawpaw, or papaya, is considered a medicinal fruit because of its high vitamin content, although it's delicious served as a dessert. It looks like a melon with smooth, orange-coloured skin and pink-tinged flesh. If ripe, serve like a melon, if underripe it can be eaten as a salad vegetable. Cook by boiling until tender and serve cold with French dressing. The flesh is watery and very thirst-quenching.

PEACH Fresh peaches are delicious in salads when they are available. Halve, stone and slice them before use. They can be skinned, if preferred. Skinning is made easier by dipping the peaches in boiling water first, but this may soften and slightly discolor the flesh. Canned peach slices need only to be drained and chopped or used whole.

PEAR Pears should be peeled, if wished, cored, sliced and tossed immediately in lemon juice to prevent discoloration.

PINEAPPLE Fresh pineapple makes a delicious salad ingredient and combines well with cheese and other savoury flavours. Trim both ends off the pineapple. Cut the whole pineapple lengthways into four or eight pieces and cut out the hard centre core from each piece. Using a sharp knife, remove the fruit from the skin, and cut out any hard 'eyes' of skin that remain. Slice or chop the fruit, as required. Alternatively, the skin can be removed from the whole fruit and the pineapple can be sliced and the core removed from each slice with a small round cutter to make pineapple rings.

The skin of a fresh pineapple can make an attractive natural dish in which to serve a salad. Simply halve the whole fruit lengthways, cutting through the leaves as well, and scoop out all the flesh with a sharp knife.

Canned pineapple pieces, cubes or chunks just need to be drained and added to a salad, and canned pineapple rings can be snipped into small pieces with scissors or used whole.

SATSUMA, TANGERINE AND CLEMENTINE When in season, these small citrus fruits can be used to add colour and flavour to salads. Simply peel and segment them, removing as much pith as possible. Canned mandarin oranges may also be drained and used if fresh fruit is not available.

DRIED FRUIT Raisins, sultanas, currants, chopped dates, prunes and apricots add sweetness and colour to a salad but should be used sparingly.

PASTA AND RICE

Pasta and rice both make ideal ingredients for a salad. They can form the base of a side salad or make a main dish salad more substantial. They can also help to extend a salad recipe—particularly useful if preparing a salad for a large number.

It is now possible to buy a wide selection of different pasta shapes, and wholewheat pastas are also readily available. All add variety to a salad. Cook pasta in boiling salted water for 10–15 minutes until tender, or as directed on the packet, then drain and rinse in cold running water and drain again.

Both long grain and brown rice can be used in salads. Long grain rice is white in colour, with only a bland, very slight flavour when cooked. Brown rice is fawn in colour when cooked and has a more chewy texture and a pleasant, nutty flavour. When rice is cooked, be it white or brown, it must be tender but should retain a slight 'bite'. The grains should be well separated.

To cook long grain rice, heat a large saucepan containing plenty of water and, when it's boiling fast, shower in the rice. Use 2.3 litres (4 pints) of water to cook 225 g (8 oz) rice and add 20 ml (4 tsp) salt to each 2.3 litres (4 pints) water. The juice of half a lemon added to the cooking water also adds flavour. Stir once to loosen any grains, then leave to bubble gently without a lid. Test for 'bite' after 12 minutes. If the rice is cooked, drain off the water, put the rice in a colander or sieve and rinse quickly under the cold tap. To add a yellow colour to the rice, for every 450 g (1 lb) rice add a pinch of saffron or about 5 ml (1 level tsp) ground turmeric to the cooking water.

Brown rice is cooked in exactly the same way as white rice but takes longer to cook—about 40 minutes—and needs more water.

When making a salad, cook any pasta or rice to be included in advance. It can be cooked in large quantities and stored in a covered container in the refrigerator for up to a week, or for several days in a cool place.

Both pasta and rice treble in weight when cooked, so use about 75 g (3 oz) cooked pasta or rice for every 25 g (1 oz) uncooked pasta or rice in a recipe.

WHOLE GRAINS

Whole wheat grain makes an ideal base for a salad. It is slightly chewy when cooked, with a delicious nutty flavour. It can be used in the same way as cooked brown or white rice (see page 18), either added to a salad or served on its own with French dressing stirred through.

Bulgar wheat (also called bulgur and burghul wheat) is whole wheat grain that has been toasted at a high temperature until the grains crack. It therefore requires little or no cooking. To serve as a side salad, soak the bulgar in cold water for 30 minutes, then drain and spread on a clean, dry tea towel. Squeeze out all the excess moisture. Place in a bowl, stir in a dressing and leave to stand for 30 minutes before serving.

NUTS, OLIVES AND SEEDS

These add texture, colour and flavour and can be stirred into a salad or used as a garnish.

NUTS Choose from walnuts, peanuts—salted or dry roasted—hazelnuts, cashews, pecans, brazils, pine nuts and almonds—blanched, flaked or toasted. They can be chopped or used whole. Add to a salad just before serving so that they remain crisp.

OLIVES The large variety of green olives, stuffed or plain, and black olives are suitable for use in salads or as a garnish.

SEEDS Poppy, caraway, sesame, sunflower and melon seeds are all suitable and are usually sprinkled on top of a salad just before serving or included in the dressing.

MAKING A MEAL OF A SALAD

When salads are to be served as a main course, they should contain some form of protein food such as meat, fish, cheese, egg or dried pulses.

MEAT Meat can be cooked specially to use in a salad, or you can use up any left-over cold meats, such as chicken, ham, turkey, beef, pork, lamb and veal. Slice or dice meat finely and add it to a salad. A variety of cooked meats and continental sliced sausages are now available from delicatessens and super-markets. Cold cooked sausages can also be sliced and used.

FISH Fresh or frozen fish can be cooked and used as a salad ingredient. Frozen shrimps and prawns are particularly delicious tossed in mayonnaise. Smoked fish, such as mackerel, is also delicious and canned tuna fish, salmon, sardines or anchovies can all be used. Serve fish salads garnished with lemon wedges.

CHEESE For salads, hard cheese can be grated, diced or sliced and soft cheeses, such as cottage and full fat, can be mixed with other ingredients or spooned on top of a salad.

EGGS Eggs are best hard-boiled and chopped, sliced or stuffed. To hard-boil eggs, place them in boiling water, bring back to the boil and boil gently for 10 minutes. They should be drained and placed at once under cold running water and the shells should be tapped immediately against the side of the pan, sink or bowl. Leave the eggs in cold water until they are cold. This prevents a discolored rim forming round the outside of the yolk and enables the shell to be removed easily. When the eggs are cold, crack the shells all round by tapping on a firm surface, then peel off the shells.

PULSES Dried beans, peas, and lentils come in all shapes, sizes and colours and, once cooked, can form the main ingredient of a salad or be mixed in with a variety of other ingredients. If they are left to marinate in a dressing for some time they soak up the flavours and are even more delicious.

Always cook more beans than you require for a dish as they can be stored in the refrigerator in a covered container for 2–3 days, and used in another salad. Canned beans can also be used for speed. They should be drained but do not require cooking.

The following chart gives approximate times for cooking 225 g (8 oz) of the more common types of pulses until tender. First soak the pulses overnight, then drain and cook in fresh water. Salt should be added at the end of the cooking time as it tends to harden the beans if added during cooking. Red kidney beans should be boiled rapidly for the first 10 minutes of their cooking, then cooked gently for a further $1-1\frac{1}{2}$ hours.

COOKING DRIED PULSES

Type	Appearance	Cooking time
Haricot beans	Kidney-shaped, pale cream	$1-1\frac{1}{2}$ hours
Flageolet beans	Kidney-shaped, pale green	1 hour
Butter beans	Large, kidney-shaped, ivory	$1\frac{1}{2}$ hours
Chick peas	Round, pointed top, ivory	$1\frac{1}{2}-2$ hours
Black-eye beans	Small, kidney-shaped, cream with black spot	45 minutes–1 hour
Red kidney beans	Kidney-shaped, red	$1-1\frac{1}{2}$ hours (boiled for first 10 minutes)
Brown kidney beans	Kidney-shaped, brown	1 hour
Black beans	Kidney-shaped, black, shiny	$1\frac{1}{2}$ hours
Aduki beans	Very small, round, red	30 minutes–1 hour
Mung (Moong) beans	Very small, round, green	40 minutes
Soya beans	Small, round, ivory, elongated when soaked	3–4 hours
Lentils	Small, red or larger greenish-brown	1 hour (no need to soak)
Split peas	Small green or yellow halved peas	45 minutes–1 hour (no need to soak)
Rose cocoa beans	Longish pink beans with darker flecks	1 hour
Cannellini beans	White, long beans	1 hour
Broad beans	Large, flat, brown	$1\frac{1}{2}-2$ hours
Foule beans	Thick skin, dull brown, about size of pea	$1-1\frac{1}{4}$ hours

PRESSURE COOKING BEANS If you have a pressure cooker, the process of cooking dried beans can be speeded up quite considerably.

Place the water in the pressure cooker. Allow at least 1.1 litres (2 pints) fresh cold water to every 450 g (1 lb) beans. The pressure cooker must be no more than half full. Bring the water to boiling point and add the beans. Bring to the boil again, uncovered, stirring frequently to prevent them sticking to the base, and remove any scum. Put on the lid, lower the heat so that the contents boil gently and bring to high (15 lb) pressure. Cook for the required time according to the chart below. Remove the cooker from the heat and reduce pressure slowly as the beans will rise and block the vent if the pressure is reduced quickly. Drain the beans and use as required.

Bean	Cooking time at high (15 lb) pressure
Haricot beans	20 minutes
Flageolet beans	20 minutes
Butter beans	25 minutes
Chick peas	20 minutes
Black-eye beans	20 minutes
Red kidney beans	20 minutes
Brown kidney beans	20 minutes
Aduki beans	10 minutes
Cannellini beans	15 minutes
Rose cocoa beans	20 minutes
Lentils	15 minutes
Split peas	15 minutes

SALAD GARNISHES

Salad garnishes are important, particularly when entertaining, as they can make all the difference to the appearance of the dish. Choose a garnish to contrast pleasantly with the salad.

CELERY CURLS Cut a celery stick into strips about 1 cm ($\frac{1}{2}$ inch) wide and 5 cm (2 inches) long. Make cuts along the length of each, close together and to within 1 cm ($\frac{1}{2}$ inch) of one end. Leave the pieces in cold or iced water for 1–2 hours, until the fringed strips curl. Drain well before using.

CUCUMBER CONES Use thin slices of cucumber. Make a cut in each slice from the centre to the outer edge, then wrap one cut edge over the other to form a cone.

CRIMPED CUCUMBER Run a fork down the sides of the cucumber to remove strips of peel, then slice the cucumber thinly in the usual way—this gives the slices an attractive deckled edge.

GHERKIN FANS Use whole gherkins, choosing long, thin ones. Cut each lengthways into thin slices, but leave them joined at one end. Fan out the strips of gherkin so that they remain just overlapping each other.

RADISH GARNISHES ROSES Choose well shaped radishes and cut a narrow slice from the top or stalk end. Cut thin snips at an angle through the skin from the stem to the root. Place the radishes in iced water for 1–2 hours and the 'petals' will open out. WATERLILIES Follow the instructions above but make four to eight small deep cuts, crossing one another across the centre of the root end and place in iced water to open out. FANS Prepare as above and make five or six deep cuts at intervals along the length of the radishes, without cutting right through. Put in iced water and leave to open like a fan.

SPRING ONION CURLS Trim the root end and all but 5 cm (2 inches) of the leaves. Skin the onion and then cut the green leaves two or three times lengthways. Place in cold water for several hours until the green leaves curl up tightly.

TOMATO LILIES Choose firm, even-sized tomatoes. Using a small, sharp-pointed knife, make a series of V-shaped cuts round the middle of each, cutting right through to the centre. Carefully pull the halves apart.

QUICK GARNISHES Sprinkle any of the following over a salad to add extra flavour and colour: Grated Cheddar cheese, Salted peanuts, Sultanas or raisins, Crisply fried pieces of bacon, Crumbled crisps, Onion rings, Sliced hard-boiled egg, Sieved egg yolk, Green or black olives, Almonds, hazelnuts or walnuts, Toasted sunflower or sesame seeds, Toasted oatmeal, Chopped fresh herbs, Lemon wedges or slices.

STARTERS
AND APPETISERS

A salad makes an ideal starter or appetiser because it can be flavoursome, yet light and not too filling. The best starter salad is simple with only a few, carefully chosen ingredients.

Salads are particularly good served before a very rich or heavy main course and, when entertaining, can be made in advance and stored in the refrigerator, allowing you more time to spend on other courses.

Salad starters can be made to look very attractive for placing on the dinner-party table. Serve avocados, halved and stoned, in special avocado dishes with the salad mixture piled on top of them. Make use of natural shells, such as scallop shells, or the scooped-out skins of melon, grapefruit or pineapple to serve salads in an attractive and impressive way.

Salad starters may be served accompanied by homemade rolls or biscuits (see page 111) or simply by thinly sliced brown bread and butter. Garnish carefully for extra appeal (see page 22).

MELON SEAFOOD SALAD

Serves 6
175 g (6 oz) skate
1 medium carrot, peeled and sliced
1 small onion, skinned and sliced
1 bay leaf
a few peppercorns
5 ml (1 tsp) white wine vinegar
salt and freshly ground pepper
125 g (4 oz) white crabmeat
15 ml (1 tbsp) lemon juice
45 ml (3 tbsp) double cream
1 small melon—Ogen, Galia or Charentais
a few lettuce leaves
lemon twists to garnish

Place the skate in a saucepan. Just cover with cold water and add the carrot, onion, bay leaf, peppercorns, vinegar and a good pinch of salt. Poach gently for about 10 minutes until the fish is just tender. Drain well, then flake the fish with a fork, discarding the skin and bone.

Flake the crabmeat and mix with the skate and lemon juice. Season with salt and pepper. Lightly whip the cream and fold into the mixture.

Cut the melon into six, scoop out the seeds and cut off the skin. Place a lettuce leaf topped with a slice of melon on six individual dishes. Spoon the fish mixture in the centre of each. Garnish with lemon twists.

LEMONY BEAN APPETISER

Serves 4
100 g (4 oz) flageolet beans, soaked
finely grated rind and juice of 1 lemon
90 ml (6 tbsp) olive oil
1 garlic clove, skinned and crushed
15 ml (1 tbsp) chopped fresh chives
salt and freshly ground pepper
225 g (8 oz) firm tomatoes, skinned

Drain the flageolet beans and cook in boiling water for about 1 hour until tender. Alternatively, cook in a pressure cooker at HIGH (15 lb) pressure for about 20 minutes. Drain well and transfer to a bowl.

Place the lemon rind, juice, oil, garlic, chives and salt and pepper in a screw-topped jar and shake well together. Pour this dressing over the warm beans, toss well and leave to cool. Cover and chill in the refrigerator.

Thinly slice the tomatoes and arrange on four individual plates or in natural scallop shells. Pile the beans and dressing, on the tomatoes.

TUNA PASTA HORS D'OEUVRE

Serves 4
75 g (3 oz) pasta shells
225 g (8 oz) small courgettes, wiped and trimmed
200-g (7-oz) can tuna fish
12 small black olives
150 ml ($\frac{1}{4}$ pint) natural yoghurt
30 ml (2 tbsp) milk
5 ml (1 level tsp) anchovy essence
15 ml (1 tbsp) lemon juice
salt and freshly ground pepper
paprika to garnish

Cook the pasta shells in boiling salted water according to packet instructions, until just tender. Meanwhile, cut the courgettes diagonally into 0.5-cm ($\frac{1}{4}$-inch) slices. Add to the boiling pasta for the last 2 minutes of the cooking time. Drain well and rinse in cold water.

Drain the tuna fish, reserving the oil, and flake the fish. Halve and stone the olives. Place the tuna oil, yoghurt, milk, anchovy essence, lemon juice and salt and pepper in a large bowl and whisk together until well combined.

Add the pasta, courgettes, tuna and olives to the dressing and stir gently to mix. Cover and chill well in the refrigerator.

MARINATED KIPPER AND AVOCADO

Serves 4
225 g (8 oz) kipper fillet, skinned
150 ml ($\frac{1}{4}$ pint) sunflower oil
60 ml (4 tbsp) lemon juice
2.5 ml ($\frac{1}{2}$ level tsp) sugar
15 ml (1 tbsp) chopped fresh parsley
25 g (1 oz) walnuts, finely chopped
salt and freshly ground pepper
1 ripe avocado

Cut the kipper fillets into thin strips 2–3 hours before needed. Place the oil, lemon juice, sugar, parsley and walnuts in a bowl and whisk together until well combined. Season well. Add the kipper and stir to ensure the dressing is evenly distributed.

Halve the avocado lengthways and remove the stone. Skin and slice the avocado, place in the bowl with the kipper and stir to coat with the dressing. Cover and leave to marinate for 2–3 hours before serving with brown bread and butter.

CRAB AND BEAN SPROUT APPETISER

Serves 6
250 g (9 oz) fresh or thawed frozen crabmeat
125 g (4 oz) fresh bean sprouts, washed
125-g (4-oz) piece cucumber, washed
60 ml (4 tbsp) mayonnaise (see page 102)
15 ml (1 tbsp) horseradish sauce
15 ml (1 tbsp) white wine vinegar
salt and freshly ground pepper
a few lettuce leaves

F lake the crabmeat and mix with the bean sprouts. Dice the cucumber and stir it into the crab mixture. In another bowl, combine the mayonnaise, horseradish sauce and vinegar, season well and add to the crab mixture. Cover and chill well in the refrigerator.

To serve, shred the lettuce leaves and arrange in the bases of six individual dishes. Stir the chilled crab mixture and spoon into the dishes.

ARTICHOKE SALAD

To avoid an overriding taste of brine, rinse the artichoke hearts and pat them dry before adding them to the salad. Omit the lemon juice if lemon-based mayonnaise is used.

Serves 6
2 eating apples
60 ml (4 level tbsp) mayonnaise (see page 102)
10–15 ml (2–3 tsp) lemon juice
10 ml (2 level tsp) horseradish sauce
2 medium tomatoes, skinned, seeded and chopped
two 400-g (14-oz) cans artichoke hearts, drained
salt and freshly ground pepper
a few lettuce leaves
paprika to garnish

P olish the apple skins with a clean dry tea towel, then quarter, core and chop the flesh. Place the mayonnaise, lemon juice and horseradish sauce in a bowl and stir to combine. Fold in the apple and tomato.

Cut the artichoke hearts into neat quarters and stir lightly into the mayonnaise mixture. Season to taste, cover and chill well in the refrigerator. Serve the salad on individual plates lined with lettuce leaves, garnished with a dusting of paprika.

CHILLED RATATOUILLE

This dish looks attractive served in natural scallop shells placed on serving plates, and garnished with plenty of chopped fresh parsley.

Serves 6
1 aubergine (about 225 g/8 oz), trimmed
salt and freshly ground pepper
450 g (1 lb) medium tomatoes
1 green pepper
125 g (4 oz) button mushrooms, wiped
about 120 ml (8 tbsp) vegetable oil
450 g (1 lb) courgettes, trimmed and thinly sliced
1 onion, skinned and sliced
100 ml (4 fl oz) red wine
30 ml (2 level tbsp) tomato purée
1 garlic clove, skinned and crushed
30 ml (2 tbsp) chopped fresh tarragon
grated Parmesan cheese
chopped fresh parsley to garnish

Cut the aubergine into small wedge-shaped pieces, place in a colander, sprinkle with salt and leave to stand for 30 minutes. Rinse well with cold water and pat dry with absorbent kitchen paper.

Skin and quarter the tomatoes, and scoop the seeds and juice into a nylon sieve placed over a bowl to catch the juice. Discard the seeds. Halve each tomato quarter lengthways and place in the bowl with the tomato juice. Cut the pepper into small diamond-shaped pieces, discarding the seeds. Halve or quarter the mushrooms.

Heat the oil in a large sauté or frying pan, add the aubergine pieces and cook until well browned, adding more oil if necessary. Lift out of the pan with a slotted spoon. Place the courgettes in the pan and fry until golden. Lift out of the pan with a slotted spoon. Fry the onion slices until lightly browned, then return the aubergines and courgettes to the pan with all the other ingredients, seasoning well. Bring to the boil, stir gently to blend, then cover, reduce the heat and simmer for 5 minutes only—the vegetables should be tender but still slightly crisp. Adjust the seasoning, spoon into a bowl and leave to cool. Cover and chill in the refrigerator.

Sprinkle with Parmesan cheese, garnish with parsley and serve well chilled with crusty French bread.

MELON AND SALAMI MAYONNAISE

Serves 6
1 medium melon (about 1.8 kg/4 lb)
4 slices coarse salami
60 ml (4 tbsp) mayonnaise (see page 102)
15 ml (1 tbsp) lemon juice
salt and freshly ground pepper
parsley sprigs to garnish

Use lightly oiled kitchen scissors to cut the salami into thin strips, then wash the blades before snipping the parsley. Quarter the melon and discard the seeds. Cut the flesh into 1-cm ($\frac{1}{2}$-inch) pieces, place in a bowl, cover and refrigerate.

Stir the salami strips into the mayonnaise with the lemon juice and seasoning to taste. Cover and place in the refrigerator.

Just before serving, drain the melon and fold into the mayonnaise and salami mixture. Spoon into six glasses, garnish with snipped parsley and serve with brown bread and butter.

MINTED PEAR VINAIGRETTE

This fresh, clean-tasting appetiser is ideal served before a main course of lamb.

Serves 6
125 g (4 oz) lean streaky bacon, rinded
135 ml (9 tbsp) French dressing (see page 100)
30 ml (2 tbsp) chopped fresh mint
3 large ripe dessert pears
1 small lettuce, washed

Grill the bacon until crisp, cool and scissor-snip into tiny pieces. Place the French dressing in a bowl or screw-topped jar with the mint and whisk or shake well together.

One at a time, peel and halve the pears and scoop out the cores with a teaspoon. Brush both sides of each pear half immediately with a little of the dressing to prevent discoloration. Cover the pears tightly with cling film until required.

To serve, arrange lettuce leaves on six individual serving plates. Place a pear half, cut-side up, on each plate and spoon over the dressing. Sprinkle with snippets of bacon.

SMOKED CHEESE AND AVOCADO SALAD

Serves 6
2 medium grapefruit
225 g (8 oz) smoked cheese
142-ml (5-fl oz) carton soured cream
salt and freshly ground pepper
3 large ripe avocados
25 g (1 oz) salted cashew nuts
paprika to garnish
a few lettuce leaves

Cut all the peel and pith away from the grapefruit using a serrated knife. Do this over a bowl to catch the juice. Divide the flesh into segments, discarding as much of the membrane as possible, and the pips. Slice the cheese into thin strips and mix with the grapefruit segments, grapefruit juice, soured cream and seasoning to taste.

Halve the avocados lengthways and remove the stones. Cut a small slice off the rounded sides of the avocado halves so that they will sit firmly on the flat plates. Pile the salad mixture into the centre of each one. Sprinkle the cashew nuts over the salad and dust lightly with paprika.

To serve, arrange lettuce leaves on six individual plates and place an avocado half on each one. As an accompaniment, serve with Cheese and Bacon Shorties given on page 121.

MELON, GRAPEFRUIT AND TOMATO SALAD

Serves 6
1 small Honeydew melon
2 grapefruit
225 g (8 oz) tomatoes
1 small piece stem ginger, finely chopped
caster sugar

Halve the melon lengthways and discard the seeds. Scoop out the melon flesh, using a melon scoop, and place in a large bowl with any juice. Using a serrated knife, remove all the skin and pith from the grapefruit. Divide the flesh into segments, discarding as much of the membrane as possible, and the pips. While doing this, hold the grapefruit over the melon bowl to catch any juice.

Skin, quarter and seed the tomatoes and, if large, halve the quarters. Add the tomatoes and ginger to the bowl and toss together, adding a little sugar if liked. Cover and chill for several hours in the refrigerator before serving in individual dishes or natural scallop shells.

DRESSED AVOCADOS

ripe avocados (allow half per person)
lemon juice
a few lettuce leaves (optional)
freshly ground black pepper, paprika or parsley sprigs to garnish

Filling alternatives: French dressing (see page 100); Tomato vinaigrette (see page 101); Garlic cream dressing (see page 104); shrimps, prawns, crab or lobster, mixed with a little thin mayonnaise or soured cream and seasoned with salt and freshly ground pepper.

Halve the avocados lengthways and remove the stones. Brush the cut surfaces of the avocados with lemon juice to prevent discoloration.

Place the avocado halves in special individual avocado dishes, or on individual serving plates lined with lettuce leaves. If serving on flat plates, cut a thin slice from the rounded side of each avocado half so that they will sit firmly on the plates.

Fill the cavities with a little of the chosen filling and garnish.

CURRIED EGG MAYONNAISE

Serves 6
50 g (2 oz) long grain rice
a pinch of ground turmeric
salt and freshly ground pepper
6 eggs, hard-boiled
30 ml (2 level tbsp) sweet pickle
30 ml (2 tbsp) lemon juice
90 ml (6 level tbsp) mayonnaise (see page 102)
10 ml (2 level tsp) concentrated curry sauce
15 ml (1 tbsp) milk
paprika and parsley sprigs to garnish

Sprinkle the rice and turmeric into a pan of boiling salted water. Cook for about 10 minutes until the rice is tender. Drain, rinse through with cold water and drain well. Spoon into the bases of six individual serving dishes.

Shell the hard-boiled eggs and cut in half lengthways. Using a teaspoon, scoop out each yolk and place in a bowl. Add the pickle, lemon juice, pepper and 1.25 ml ($\frac{1}{4}$ level tsp) salt. Cream together, then spoon the mixture into the egg whites.

Arrange two of the egg halves, cut-side down, on each dish of rice. Combine the mayonnaise with the curry sauce and milk and spoon over the eggs to mask. Garnish with a line of paprika and parsley sprigs.

SALAMI ANTIPASTA

Serves 2
50 g (2 oz) pasta shapes
100 g (4 oz) salami
½ red pepper
½ green pepper
18 black olives
30 ml (2 tbsp) French dressing (see page 100)

Cook the pasta shapes in boiling salted water for 9–10 minutes until tender. Drain and leave to cool. Cut the salami into strips using lightly oiled kitchen scissors. Remove the cores and seeds from the pepper halves and slice into fine strips. Halve and stone the olives.

Place the pasta, salami, peppers and olives in a bowl. Add the French dressing and toss together. Serve on individual plates.

PRAWN COCKTAIL

Serves 4
60 ml (4 tbsp) mayonnaise (see page 102)
60 ml (4 tbsp) single cream
10 ml (2 tsp) tomato purée
10 ml (2 tsp) lemon juice
a dash of Worcestershire sauce
a dash of dry sherry
salt and freshly ground pepper
225 g (8 oz) peeled prawns
a few lettuce leaves, shredded
lemon slices to garnish

In a small bowl, mix together the mayonnaise, cream, tomato purée, lemon juice, Worcestershire sauce and sherry. Season to taste. Add the prawns and stir well to coat.

Place shredded lettuce into four glasses and top with the prawn mixture. Garnish each glass with a lemon slice. Serve with triangles of thinly sliced brown bread and butter.

CHOUFLEUR VINAIGRETTE

Serves 6
800 g (1¾ lb) cauliflower, trimmed
1 egg
90 ml (6 tbsp) French dressing (see page 100)
a few flaked almonds, toasted or a few anchovies, chopped, to garnish

Break the cauliflower into tiny florets. Cook, covered, in 2.5 cm (1 inch) of boiling salted water for 5 minutes. Drain at once and place the cauliflower in a serving dish.

Cook the egg in boiling water for 3 minutes. Place the French dressing in a bowl.

Shell the egg and press it through a sieve into the dressing. Pour the dressing over the cauliflower, toss well together, cover and chill in the refrigerator until required. Just before serving, scatter the almonds or anchovies on top.

STUFFED EGG MAYONNAISE

Illustrated in colour opposite

Serves 4
4 eggs, hard-boiled
75 g (3 oz) Blue Brie (Cambozola)
75 g (3 oz) full fat soft cheese
45–60 ml (3–4 tbsp) single cream
salt and freshly ground pepper
225 g (8 oz) tomatoes, skinned
150 ml (¼ pint) mayonnaise (see page 102)
parsley sprigs to garnish

Halve the eggs lengthways, scoop out the yolks and press them through a sieve. Rinse the egg whites in cold water and carefully dry them on absorbent kitchen paper. Cut the rind off the Brie, place the cheese in a bowl and beat until smooth. Work in the full fat soft cheese with the sieved egg yolks, cream and seasoning, beating until smooth and of a piping consistency. Spoon the cream cheese mixture into a piping bag fitted with a 1-cm (½-inch) star nozzle and pipe swirls of the mixture into the egg whites.

Slice half the tomatoes and arrange in four individual serving dishes. Place two stuffed egg halves on each and refrigerate for 30 minutes. Halve, seed and roughly chop the remaining tomatoes and stir into the mayonnaise. Spoon a little mayonnaise over each egg and garnish with parsley sprigs.

Clockwise from top: Prawn cauliflower salad (*page 43*); Stuffed egg mayonnaise (*page 32*) and Brown bread sticks (*page 114*).

Clockwise from top: Platter hors d'oeuvre (*page 44*); Garlic bread (*page 114*) and Mozzarella salad (*page 40*).

BEAN AND HADDOCK APPETISER

A fresh, cool and colourful starter that can be
prepared ahead.

Serves 6
50 g (2 oz) red kidney beans, soaked overnight
1 small bunch watercress
135 ml (9 tbsp) French dressing (see page 100)
4 sticks celery, trimmed and thinly sliced
275 g (10 oz) fresh haddock fillet
1 bay leaf
6 peppercorns
salt

Drain the kidney beans and place them in a saucepan. Cover the beans with fresh water, bring to the boil and boil for 10 minutes, then simmer, covered, for about 1 hour until tender.

Meanwhile, wash the watercress well, drain and finely chop some of the sprigs to give about 60 ml (4 tbsp). Pat the remaining sprigs dry with absorbent kitchen paper and store in a polythene bag in the refrigerator until required. Place the French dressing in a bowl and stir in the chopped watercress and the celery.

Place the haddock in a shallow saucepan with enough water to cover. Add the bay leaf, peppercorns and salt and bring to the boil. Cover and simmer gently for about 10 minutes, until the fish is beginning to flake. Drain off the liquid and divide the fish into bite-sized pieces, discarding the skin and bones. Add to the dressing with the beans while both retain a little of their cooking heat. When cold, cover and chill well in the refrigerator. Arrange on individual plates, garnish with the remaining watercress sprigs, and serve with oatcakes or crispbread.

ONION AND TOMATO SALAD

Serves 4
4 medium tomatoes, skinned and very thinly sliced
2 medium onions, skinned and very thinly sliced
10 ml (2 tsp) snipped fresh chives
45 ml (3 tbsp) French dressing (see page 100)

Arrange the tomato and onion slices alternately in a shallow dish. Add the chives to the French dressing, mix well and pour over the salad. Cover and chill well in the refrigerator. Serve with Cheese straws (see page 119).

AVOCADO APPETISER

The smooth, creamy texture of avocado contrasts nicely with crisp, juicy apples.

Serves 4
2 crisp green eating apples
juice of $\frac{1}{2}$ lemon
1 avocado
a few lettuce leaves or a few sprigs of watercress
90 ml (6 tbsp) French dressing (see page 100)
chopped fresh parsley to garnish

Quarter and core the apples and peel them, if preferred. Slice the apples thinly and toss them in the lemon juice.

Halve, stone, peel and slice the avocado and add to the apple. Arrange lettuce leaves or watercress on four individual serving plates and spoon the avocado mixture on top. Pour a little dressing over and garnish with parsley.

SAVOURY EGGS WITH STILTON

Danish Mycella cheese makes a very pleasant alternative to Stilton in this attractive savoury.

Serves 6
50 g (2 oz) butter, softened
125 g (4 oz) Stilton cheese, crumbled
45 ml (3 tbsp) single cream
6 eggs, hard-boiled
50 g (2 oz) walnut pieces
2 sticks celery, trimmed and very finely chopped
salt and freshly ground pepper
watercress sprigs to garnish

Beat the butter until quite smooth and gradually work in the cheese and the cream. Shell the eggs and halve them lengthways. Scoop out the yolks and press them through a sieve into the cheese mixture. Place the egg whites in a bowl of cold water until required.

Finely chop half the walnuts and beat them into the cheese mixture with the celery. Season to taste. Spoon the mixture into a piping bag fitted with a 1-cm ($\frac{1}{2}$-inch) plain nozzle. Drain the egg whites and pat them dry with absorbent kitchen paper. Pipe the cheese filling into the centre of each. Arrange the eggs side-by-side around the edge of a shallow-rimmed serving dish and sprinkle with the remaining walnut pieces. Cover and chill.

Take out of the refrigerator 30 minutes before serving. Fill the centre of the dish with watercress sprigs and serve with French bread or crispy bread rolls.

MARINATED MUSHROOMS

Serves 4–6
450 g (1 lb) small button mushrooms, wiped
150 ml ($\frac{1}{4}$ pint) French dressing (see page 100)
chopped fresh parsley to garnish

Place the mushrooms in a bowl and pour over the French dressing. Cover and leave to marinate in the refrigerator for 6–8 hours, stirring occasionally. Serve in individual shallow dishes, sprinkled with chopped parsley. Accompany with rolled brown bread and butter or garlic bread (see page 114).

SEAKALE SALAD

Serves 4
750 g (1$\frac{1}{2}$ lb) seakale, washed and trimmed
lemon juice
For the dressing:
90 ml (6 tbsp) vegetable oil
45 ml (3 tbsp) lemon juice
1 garlic clove, skinned and crushed
salt and freshly ground pepper

Cut the seakale into 5-cm (2-inch) lengths and cook in boiling salted water, with a little lemon juice added, for 4–5 minutes. Drain well, pressing out any surplus water, and place the seakale in a serving dish.

Place all the dressing ingredients in a bowl or screw-topped jar and whisk or shake well together. Pour the dressing over the seakale and toss until evenly coated. Chill well in the refrigerator for 1–2 hours or overnight.

CARROT AND ORANGE SALAD

Serves 4
450 g (1 lb) carrots, peeled
grated rind and juice of 1 orange
25 g (1 oz) sultanas
15 g ($\frac{1}{2}$ oz) hazelnuts, roughly chopped
135 ml (9 tbsp) French dressing (see page 100)

Grate the carrots into a salad bowl and add the orange rind, sultanas and hazelnuts. Combine the orange juice with the dressing and toss well into the salad. Cover and chill in the refrigerator before serving.

STUFFED APPLE APPETISER

Serves 4
4 large eating apples
juice of 1 lemon
100 g (4 oz) cottage cheese
25 g (1 oz) pecan nuts, chopped
200-g (7-oz) can tuna fish, drained and flaked
30 ml (2 tbsp) white wine vinegar
15 ml (1 tbsp) salad oil
salt and freshly ground pepper
chopped fresh parsley to garnish

Cut a slice from the top of each apple and remove the centres with a sharp knife or apple corer. Carefully scoop out as much flesh from each apple as possible, leaving a firm shell. Brush the inside of the apples with lemon juice. Quickly chop the apple flesh and combine it with the cheese, nuts and tuna. Place the vinegar and oil in a bowl or screw-topped jar and whisk or shake well together. Use this dressing to moisten the tuna mixture, then adjust the seasoning. Pile the mixture into the apples, garnish with parsley and serve immediately.

BROCCOLI MAYONNAISE

Like asparagus, this fragile vegetable needs to be cooked with care. It's tender when the point of a knife pierces the stem with just a little resistance.

Serves 6
450 g (1 lb) fresh broccoli
1 egg, hard-boiled
25 g (1 oz) dry roasted peanuts, chopped
300 ml ($\frac{1}{2}$ pint) mayonnaise (see page 102)

Trim away any thick broccoli stalks, then divide the heads into medium-sized florets. Rinse well. Blanch the broccoli in boiling salted water for 3–4 minutes only—it should still retain its crispness. Thoroughly drain, leave to cool, then refrigerate.

   Shell and roughly chop the egg and mix with the peanuts. To serve, arrange the broccoli on individual plates. Spoon over a little mayonnaise, without completely masking the vegetable, and sprinkle with the egg mixture. Serve with fingers of hot toast.

AVOCADO AND RED BEAN SALAD

Pale green flageolet beans—a variety of haricot—are an attractive alternative to red kidney beans, but they're not always easy to find.

Serves 6
90 ml (6 tbsp) French dressing (see page 100)
2 ripe avocados
432-g (15¼-oz) can red kidney beans
a few lettuce leaves, shredded

Place the French dressing in a bowl. Halve the avocados lengthways, remove the stones and carefully pull or cut off the skins. Slice the avocado flesh into small fork-sized pieces. Immediately add the avocado to the dressing and stir gently until well coated.

Drain the beans, rinse them in cold water and drain again. Stir the beans gently into the avocado mixture, cover tightly with cling film and refrigerate for 2 hours.

Before serving, give the salad a gentle stir. Arrange on small plates lined with shredded lettuce and serve with a basket of sliced oven-warmed French bread.

TUNA BEAN SALAD

If flageolet beans are difficult to come by, use red kidney beans, and use chopped parsley instead of paprika as a garnish.

Serves 6
198-g (7-oz) can tuna fish
439-g (15¼-oz) can green flageolet beans, drained
2 medium oranges
salt and freshly ground pepper
1 small lettuce
56-g (2-oz) packet cashew nuts, roughly chopped
paprika to garnish

Place the tuna with the can oil in a bowl and break into fork-sized pieces. Add the beans to the bowl. Using a serrated knife, carefully remove all the peel and pith from the oranges. Divide the oranges into segments and add to the bowl with any juice. Season well and stir lightly to mix the ingredients. Cover and chill in the refrigerator for several hours.

Arrange the lettuce on individual serving plates. Stir the cashew nuts into the salad ingredients and spoon the mixture on top of the lettuce. Before serving, dust with paprika to garnish.

FLORIDA CHICORY SALAD

A greenish tinge at the top of chicory heads
usually means they'll taste bitter. Select those
tinged with yellow.

Serves 6
1 small grapefruit
2 oranges
225 g (8 oz) tomatoes
225 g (8 oz) chicory
30 ml (2 tbsp) vegetable oil
15 ml (1 tbsp) lemon juice
10 ml (2 level tsp) soft light brown sugar
salt and freshly ground pepper
45 ml (3 tbsp) chopped fresh parsley

Using a serrated knife, cut away all the peel and pith from the grapefruit
and oranges and divide the flesh into segments, discarding as much of the
membrane as possible, and the pips. Prepare the fruit over a bowl to catch any
juice, then add the segments to the bowl.

Skin and quarter the tomatoes, scooping the seeds and juice into a nylon
sieve placed over the bowl to catch any juice. Discard the seeds. If large, slice
the tomato quarters into eighths and add to the bowl.

Trim off the root and wash the chicory, removing any outer damaged
leaves. Slice diagonally into 1-cm ($\frac{1}{2}$-inch) pieces. Open out the slices and add
to the tomato, grapefruit and orange mixture.

Place the oil, lemon juice, sugar, seasoning and parsley in a bowl or
screw-topped jar and whisk or shake well together. Pour over the fruit and
vegetable mixture and stir well. Adjust the seasoning and, if the fruit is very
acidic, add a little more sugar. Cover the bowl and chill well in the
refrigerator. Serve with slices of hot herb bread (see page 114).

TOMATO SALAD WITH BASIL

Serves 6
750 g (1$\frac{1}{2}$ lb) ripe tomatoes, skinned
135 ml (9 tbsp) olive oil
45 ml (3 tbsp) wine vinegar
1 small garlic clove, skinned and crushed
30 ml (2 tbsp) chopped fresh basil
salt and freshly ground pepper

Slice the tomatoes thinly and arrange on six individual serving plates. Place
the oil, vinegar, garlic, basil and seasoning in a bowl or screw-topped jar and
whisk or shake well together. Spoon over the tomatoes. Cover the plates
tightly with cling film and chill in the refrigerator for about 2 hours. Serve the
salad with fresh brown rolls or bread and butter.

MARINATED COURGETTE AND MUSHROOM SALAD

Serves 6
25 g (1 oz) shelled hazelnuts
½ green pepper, seeded and chopped
60 ml (4 tbsp) dry white wine
15 ml (1 tbsp) lemon juice
30 ml (2 tbsp) chopped fresh chervil
salt and freshly ground pepper
75 ml (5 tbsp) vegetable oil
450 g (1 lb) courgettes, trimmed and thinly sliced
175 g (6 oz) button mushrooms, wiped and thickly sliced

Roast the nuts in a hot oven or under the grill until well browned. Place them in a clean tea towel and rub off the skins. Allow the nuts to cool and then chop roughly. Place the green pepper and nuts in a large bowl with the wine, lemon juice, chervil and seasoning.

Heat the oil in a large frying pan and sauté the courgettes quickly, a few at a time, until well browned. Do not overcook them—they should still be slightly crisp. Drain off the oil and, while still warm, add it to the bowl with the courgettes. Fry the mushrooms in the residual oil in the pan for a few seconds only, then tip the contents of the pan into the bowl. Stir well to mix, then leave to cool, stirring gently from time to time. Cover and chill well in the refrigerator before serving in individual shallow dishes accompanied by Wholemeal scone fingers (see page 120) and butter.

MEXICAN BEAN APPETISER

Serves 6
432-g (15¼-oz) can red kidney beans, drained
4 sticks celery, trimmed and chopped
25 g (1 oz) gherkins, chopped
30 ml (2 level tbsp) finely chopped onion
90 ml (6 tbsp) French dressing (see page 100)
2 eggs, hard-boiled
1 Cos lettuce
a few celery leaves (optional)

Place the kidney beans in a bowl, add the chopped celery, gherkin and onion and mix together. Pour over the French dressing and mix well.

Shell and slice the eggs lengthways. Arrange lettuce leaves on six individual plates and pile the bean mixture on top. Spoon over any remaining dressing. Place slices of hard-boiled egg on each and add a few celery leaves either side.

ARTICHOKE AND MUSHROOM SALAD

Serves 6
125 g (4 oz) button mushrooms, wiped
3 spring onions
grated rind and juice of 1 small orange
salt and freshly ground pepper
two 400-g (14-oz) cans artichoke hearts, drained

To give the mushroom and onion dressing a little more body, whisk 10 ml (2 tsp) vegetable oil into the orange juice. Chop the mushrooms well. Trim and finely chop the spring onions. Strain 60 ml (4 tbsp) orange juice into a bowl and add the orange rind and plenty of seasoning. Add the chopped vegetables, cover and refrigerate for about 2 hours. Cut each artichoke heart into four pieces and place on six individual serving plates. Cover with cling film and refrigerate until needed.

Just before serving, give the mushroom mixture another stir and spoon over the artichoke hearts. Serve with Melba toast (see page 114).

MOZZARELLA SALAD

Illustrated in colour facing page 33

Serves 4
2 ripe avocados
120 ml (8 tbsp) French dressing (see page 100)
175 g (6 oz) Mozzarella cheese, thinly sliced
4 medium tomatoes, thinly sliced
chopped fresh parsley and mint to garnish

Halve the avocados lengthways and remove the stones. Peel and cut the avocados into slices. Pour the French dressing over the avocado. Stir to coat thoroughly and prevent discoloration.

Arrange slices of Mozzarella, tomato and avocado on four individual serving plates. Spoon over the dressing and sprinkle with chopped herbs.

ARTICHOKE VINAIGRETTE

Serves 6
6 globe artichokes
1 lemon
For the dressing:
1 egg, hard-boiled
200 ml (7 fl oz) olive oil
100 ml (4 fl oz) white wine vinegar
1 small onion, skinned and finely chopped
30 ml (2 tbsp) chopped fresh parsley
30 ml (2 tbsp) snipped chives
salt and freshly ground pepper

Break the tough outer leaves (scales) off the artichokes, then cut off the stems quite close to the base leaves. Trim the spiky tops of the leaves with kitchen scissors and rub the artichokes with a piece of lemon to prevent discoloration. Soak the artichokes in cold salted water for 30 minutes or wash thoroughly in cold running water.

Meanwhile, prepare the dressing. Shell and finely chop the egg. Place 175 ml (6 fl oz) oil, the vinegar, onion, egg, herbs and seasonings in a bowl or screw-topped jar and whisk or shake well together. Chill in the refrigerator until required.

Cook the artichokes in a large pan of boiling salted water with the remaining oil and a squeeze of lemon juice for 30–40 minutes. When cooked, a leaf will easily pull away from the stem. Turn the artichokes upside-down in a colander to drain. Scoop out the chokes, the mass of yellowish hairs at the centre of the artichoke. Place the artichokes on individual serving plates and serve with brown bread and butter. Whisk or shake the dressing and serve separately.

MELON AND PARMA HAM

Serves 6
½ large Honeydew melon, chilled
6 thin slices Parma ham
juice of 1 lemon
freshly ground pepper
lemon wedges to garnish

Scoop out and discard the seeds from the melon. Cut the melon lengthways into six sections and cut the flesh from the skin with a sharp knife.

Place one piece of melon on each slice of ham and wrap the ham round the melon. Place on individual serving plates and sprinkle with lemon juice and pepper. Serve garnished with lemon wedges and accompanied by brown bread and butter.

STUFFED TOMATOES

Serves 4
4 large tomatoes
1 small red pepper, halved and seeded
125 g (4 oz) mushrooms, wiped
15 ml (1 tbsp) vegetable oil
4 spring onions, trimmed and finely chopped
salt and freshly ground pepper
90 ml (6 tbsp) mayonnaise (see page 102)
parsley sprigs to garnish
a few lettuce leaves

Cut the tops off the tomatoes, scoop out the flesh using a teaspoon, and discard. Roughly chop the tops and put them in a bowl. Sprinkle the insides of the tomatoes with salt, turn upside-down and leave to drain.

Finely chop the pepper and mushrooms. Heat the oil in a frying pan, add the pepper and mushrooms and sauté for about 5 minutes until soft. Remove from the pan, drain on absorbent kitchen paper and add them to the bowl with the onions. Season well. Add the mayonnaise and mix well. Spoon the mixture into the tomato cases and garnish with parsley sprigs. Place on lettuce leaves on individual serving plates.

AVOCADO WITH CITRUS DRESSING

Serves 6
1 medium juicy grapefruit
1 small bunch spring onions, trimmed and finely chopped
150 ml ($\frac{1}{4}$ pint) vegetable oil
2.5 ml ($\frac{1}{2}$ level tsp) caster sugar
salt and freshly ground pepper
3 ripe avocados
paprika to garnish

Halve the grapefruit and squeeze out the juice. Strain 105 ml (7 tbsp) of the juice and place it in a bowl or screw-topped jar with the onions, oil, sugar and seasoning. Whisk or shake well, then cover and refrigerate for at least 1 hour.

Just before serving, halve the avocados and remove the stones. Brush a little of the dressing over the cut surfaces of the avocados to prevent discoloration. Place the avocado halves in special avocado dishes or have a small portion off the rounded side of each one so that they will sit firmly on flat serving plates. Give the dressing another good shake and spoon some into the hollow of each avocado. Dust with paprika and serve with fingers of warm toast.

PRAWN CAULIFLOWER SALAD

Illustrated in colour facing page 32

Serves 6
90 ml (6 tbsp) mayonnaise (see page 102)
15 ml (1 level tbsp) tomato purée
15 ml (1 tbsp) sherry
30 ml (2 tbsp) lemon juice
salt and freshly ground pepper
1 small cauliflower, trimmed (about 450 g/1lb trimmed weight)
125 g (4 oz) cucumber
125 g (4 oz) frozen prawns, thawed
1 small endive, trimmed
chopped fresh parsley to garnish (optional)

In a large bowl, mix the mayonnaise with the tomato purée, sherry, lemon juice and salt and pepper to taste. Break the cauliflower into tiny florets, blanch in boiling salted water for 2 minutes, then drain well. While still warm, stir the cauliflower into the mayonnaise mixture, then leave to cool.

Dice the cucumber, place in a colander and sprinkle lightly with salt. Leave for about 20 minutes, then drain, rinse and drain again. Stir the cucumber into the cauliflower mixture with the prawns. Cover and chill in the refrigerator. Line six natural scallop shells with endive leaves and pile the salad on top. Serve garnished with parsley.

CHILLED CAULIFLOWER WITH LEMON DRESSING

Serves 4
450 g (1 lb) cauliflower, trimmed
finely grated rind of $\frac{1}{2}$ lemon
45 ml (3 tbsp) lemon juice
120 ml (8 tbsp) vegetable oil
salt and freshly ground pepper
1.25 ml ($\frac{1}{4}$ level tsp) dried oregano or marjoram
1 small green pepper, seeded and chopped
1 cap of canned pimento, chopped
1 garlic clove, skinned

Break the cauliflower into small florets. Cook in 2.5 cm (1 inch) of boiling salted water for about 3 minutes. Drain, rinse in cold water and drain again. Turn the cauliflower into a serving dish.

Place the ingredients in a bowl or screw-topped jar, whisk or shake well together and pour the dressing over the cauliflower. Leave at room temperature for 2–3 hours. Remove the garlic clove before serving.

ASPARAGUS AND EGG MAYONNAISE

Serves 4
350–450 g (12 oz–1 lb) asparagus, trimmed
4 eggs, hard-boiled
60 ml (4 tbsp) double cream
5 ml (1 level tsp) tomato purée
15 ml (1 tbsp) sherry
5 ml (1 tsp) lemon juice
salt and freshly ground white pepper
150 ml ($\frac{1}{4}$ pint) mayonnaise (see page 102)
paprika to garnish

Tie the asparagus in bundles of six to eight stalks. Stand them upright in a pan of boiling salted water and cook for 10–15 minutes until tender. Drain well, remove the ties and cool. Reserve eight asparagus tips for garnish. Chop the remainder and arrange in the base of four individual dishes.

Shell and cut the eggs in half lengthways and arrange, cut-side down, on the asparagus. Stir the cream, tomato purée, sherry, lemon juice and seasoning into the mayonnaise and spoon over the eggs. Garnish with the reserved asparagus tips and dust lightly with paprika.

PLATTER HORS D'OEUVRE

Illustrated in colour facing page 33

Serves 6
50 g (2 oz) sliced salami
99-g ($3\frac{1}{2}$-oz) can tuna fish, drained
200-g (7-oz) can pimentos, drained
106-g ($3\frac{3}{4}$-oz) can brislings in olive oil, drained
106-g ($3\frac{3}{4}$-oz) can shrimps, drained
1 crisp lettuce heart
12 black olives
12 stuffed olives
radishes
90 ml (6 tbsp) garlic dressing (see page 104)

Remove the rind from the salami, if necessary. Halve each slice and curl into a cornet. Flake the tuna fish chunkily and slice the pimentos into strips. On a flat platter, arrange the salami, tuna, pimento strips, brisling, shrimps and lettuce. Cover tightly with cling film and chill in the refrigerator for several hours.

About 1 hour before serving, add the olives and radishes. Spoon over the dressing, cover and chill again. Serve with chunks of French bread or garlic bread (see page 114).

MAIN-COURSE SALADS

A salad soon becomes a complete meal in itself with the addition of meat, eggs, cheese, fish or dried pulses. It is an ideal way of using up left-over cold cooked meat and main course salads make excellent informal supper or lunch dishes.

Serve these more elaborate and substantial salads with a simple side salad, or just with some crusty French bread and butter. Alternatively, choose one of the more unusual roll or biscuit recipes from Chapter 6 (page 111), such as Hot mustard finger rolls or Cheese and bacon shorties.

Salads can be made more substantial by adding some cold cooked rice or pasta. This is helpful when cooking for large numbers, such as for a buffet party, as extra rice or pasta will help a salad go round more people.

The beauty of a main-course salad is that it can be made quickly and easily, and often from ingredients that you already have in the refrigerator, freezer or store-cupboard.

GINGERED CHICKEN AND MELON SALAD

Serves 4
1.4-kg (3-lb) oven-ready chicken
1 onion slice
1 carrot, peeled and sliced
6 peppercorns
1 bay leaf
60 ml (4 tbsp) French dressing (see page 100)
15 g ($\frac{1}{2}$ oz) butter
1 small onion, skinned and finely chopped
2.5 ml ($\frac{1}{2}$ level tsp) ground ginger
1.25 ml ($\frac{1}{4}$ level tsp) paprika
50 g (2 oz) celery, finely chopped
25 g (1 oz) stem ginger, finely chopped
60 ml (4 tbsp) soured cream
60 ml (4 tbsp) mayonnaise (see page 102)
1 medium ripe Honeydew melon
chopped fresh parsley to garnish

A day ahead, place the chicken in a large saucepan, add the onion slice, carrot, peppercorns and bay leaf and cover with cold water. Cover the pan, bring to a boil, reduce the heat and simmer for about $1\frac{1}{4}$ hours until the chicken is tender. Leave the chicken to cool in the cooking liquid. When cold, remove the chicken from the pan and cut all the meat from the carcass. Place the meat in a large bowl, pour over the French dressing and leave to marinate overnight.

The next day, heat the butter in a pan and sauté the onion for 2 minutes. Add the ginger and paprika and cook for a further minute. Transfer to a bowl and leave to cool. Add the celery, stem ginger, soured cream and mayonnaise and mix well.

About 30 minutes before serving, halve the melon and discard the seeds. Using a grapefruit knife, scoop out all the flesh and roughly chop. Add it to the other ingredients with the drained chicken, and toss gently. Chill slightly in the refrigerator. Pile the salad on to a serving dish or back into the melon shell, and garnish with chopped parsley.

TWO-BEAN SAUSAGE SALAD

Serves 4–6
125 g (4 oz) dried black-eye beans, soaked overnight
225 g (8 oz) French beans, topped and tailed
45 ml (3 tbsp) French dressing (see page 100)
175 g (6 oz) white grapes
240 g (8½ oz) smoked pork sausage
75 g (3 oz) Dolcelatte or Gorgonzola cheese
150 ml (¼ pint) single cream
freshly ground black pepper
paprika to garnish

Drain the black-eye beans and put in a saucepan. Cover with fresh water, bring to the boil, cover and simmer gently for about 30 minutes until tender. Drain and tip into a large bowl.

Break the French beans in half. Boil in salted water for about 8 minutes until just tender. Drain and mix with the black-eye beans. While the beans are still warm, pour the French dressing over and stir to combine. Leave to cool.

Halve and pip the grapes and thinly slice the sausage. Stir into the cold bean mixture, cover and chill well in the refrigerator.

Mash the cheese with a fork and combine with the cream and plenty of black pepper. Stir into the salad just before serving. Garnish with a light dusting of paprika.

SMOKED MACKEREL SALAD

Serves 4
450 g (1 lb) small new potatoes
350 g (12 oz) smoked mackerel fillets
142-ml (5-fl oz) carton soured cream
60 ml (4 level tbsp) mayonnaise (see page 102)
45 ml (3 level tbsp) horseradish sauce
salt and freshly ground pepper
225 g (8 oz) celery, trimmed and sliced
paprika to garnish
lemon wedges to serve

Cook the potatoes in their skins in boiling salted water for 10–15 minutes until tender. Drain, peel off the skins, halve and leave to cool. Skin the mackerel fillets and divide the flesh into fork-sized pieces.

In a large bowl, mix the soured cream with the mayonnaise, horseradish and seasoning. Stir in the fish, celery and potatoes, cover and chill well in the refrigerator. Serve the salad sprinkled with paprika and accompanied by lemon wedges.

SPINACH AND AVOCADO SALAD

Illustrated in colour opposite

Serves 4
350 g (12 oz) spinach
125 g (4 oz) streaky bacon, rinded
125 g (4 oz) Caerphilly cheese
2 medium ripe avocados
50 g (2 oz) spring onions, trimmed
For the dressing
45 ml (3 tbsp) salad oil
15 ml (1 tbsp) white wine vinegar
2.5 ml ($\frac{1}{2}$ level tsp) dried oregano
15 ml (1 tbsp) snipped fresh chives

W ash the spinach well, remove the central stalks and pull into pieces. Grill the bacon until crisp, cool and snip into small pieces. Cut the cheese into 1-cm ($\frac{1}{2}$-inch) cubes. Halve the avocados lengthways and remove the stones. Peel and thinly slice the avocado flesh. Finely scissor-snip the spring onions.

Place all the dressing ingredients in a bowl or screw-topped jar and whisk or shake well together. Put all the salad ingredients in a bowl, pour over the dressing and toss lightly.

MARINATED BEEF SALAD

Serves 4
225 g (8 oz) bean sprouts
350 g (12 oz) cooked medium rare roast beef
1 medium onion, skinned and thinly sliced
125 g (4 oz) green pepper, seeded
125 g (4 oz) celery, trimmed
175 g (6 oz) carrot, peeled
60 ml (4 tbsp) sherry
30 ml (2 tbsp) soy sauce
15 ml (1 tbsp) red wine vinegar
30 ml (2 tbsp) thin honey
salt and freshly ground pepper

W ash the bean sprouts and drain thoroughly. Shred the beef and combine with the bean sprouts and onion. Finely slice the green pepper, celery and carrot and add to the beef mixture.

Combine the sherry, soy sauce, vinegar and honey in a bowl and stir well until the honey blends in. Pour this dressing over the beef and vegetables, add plenty of seasoning and stir well. Cover and leave in the refrigerator overnight. To serve, toss the salad and turn on to a serving dish.

Clockwise from top: Moulded kipper and egg ring (*page 60*); Spinach and avocado salad (*recipe opposite*) and Melba toast (*page 114*).

Sausage and bean salad (*page 66*).

LIVER SAUSAGE AND CAULIFLOWER SALAD

Serves 4
1 medium cauliflower, trimmed
125 g (4 oz) button mushrooms
90 ml (6 tbsp) vegetable oil
30 ml (2 tbsp) distilled malt vinegar
30 ml (2 level tbsp) French mustard
salt and freshly ground pepper
275–350 g (10–12 oz) firm unsliced liver sausage
2 caps canned pimento, drained
chopped fresh parsley to garnish

Break the cauliflower into small florets. Wipe the mushrooms and quarter any that are on the large side. Place the oil, vinegar, mustard and seasoning in a bowl or screw-topped jar and whisk or shake together.

Blanch the cauliflower in boiling salted water for 2 minutes, then drain quickly. While still warm, transfer the cauliflower to a bowl with the mushrooms and pour over the dressing. Toss well, then leave to cool. Stir occasionally until most of the dressing is absorbed and the cauliflower is cold.

Cut the sausage into fork-sized cubes and dice the pimento. Mix both into the salad, cover and chill well in the refrigerator. To serve, pile into a salad bowl and garnish with chopped parsley.

SAUSAGE SLAW

Serves 4
450 g (1 lb) pork sausages
212-g (7½-oz) can butter beans, drained
225 g (8 oz) celery, trimmed and chopped
175 g (6 oz) white cabbage, finely sliced
75 g (3 oz) sultanas
1 garlic clove, skinned and crushed
30 ml (2 tbsp) olive or corn oil
15 ml (1 tbsp) white wine vinegar
1.25 ml (¼ level tsp) celery seed
salt and freshly ground pepper

Grill or fry the sausages until evenly browned, drain well and allow to cool. When cold, cut into slices.

Place the beans, celery, cabbage, sultanas and sliced sausages in a bowl and toss together. Place the remaining ingredients in a bowl or screw-topped jar and whisk or shake well together. Pour over the salad. Toss the salad with the dressing to coat evenly. Leave for about 30 minutes to mellow.

SPICED DUCK AND ORANGE SALAD

Serves 4
1.8-kg (4-lb) oven-ready duckling
2 oranges
salt and freshly ground pepper
45 ml (3 tbsp) vegetable oil
15 ml (1 tbsp) white wine vinegar
30 ml (2 tbsp) mayonnaise (see page 102)
10 ml (2 level tsp) curry powder
30 ml (2 level tbsp) orange marmalade
125 g (4 oz) podded peas, cooked
snipped fresh chives or chopped parsley to garnish

Preheat the oven to 180°C (350°F) mark 4. Wipe the duckling and prick well all over with a fork. Using a potato peeler or sharp knife, pare the rind from one orange and place it inside the duckling. Place the duckling on a rack or trivet in a roasting tin, sprinkle with salt and roast in the oven for about 2 hours, or until the juices run clear and the flesh is tender. While still warm, strip the breast skin off the duck and reserve. Carve off all the meat and shred finely.

In a large bowl, mix the oil, vinegar, mayonnaise, curry powder and marmalade and season with salt and pepper. Stir in the duck. Using a serrated knife, remove all the peel and pith from the oranges and divide into segments, discarding as much of the membrane as possible, and the pips. Add to the duck with the cold cooked peas. Cover and refrigerate.

Cut the reserved duck skin into strips and grill until crisp. Just before serving, use to garnish the salad, then scissor-snip chives directly over the salad.

PIQUANT HAM, BROAD BEAN AND PASTA SALAD

Serves 4
125 g (4 oz) pasta twists
450 g (1 lb) frozen or fresh broad beans, podded
150 ml ($\frac{1}{4}$ pint) mayonnaise (see page 102)
45 ml (3 level tbsp) finely chopped onion
142-ml (5-fl oz) carton soured cream
salt and freshly ground pepper
225 g (8 oz) sliced ham, diced
a few chives
paprika to garnish

Cook the pasta twists in boiling salted water for 10–15 minutes until tender. Drain well. Rinse in cold water to cool quickly and drain again. Cook the broad beans in boiling salted water for about 15 minutes until tender. Drain well and rinse in cold water to cool quickly. Drain and pat dry on absorbent kitchen paper. Place the mayonnaise, onion and soured cream in a bowl, stir to combine, then season to taste.

In a bowl, combine the pasta twists, broad beans and ham. Add the mayonnaise mixture and stir lightly. Scissor-snip some chives into the salad. Pile into a serving dish and sprinkle with paprika. Chill in the refrigerator before serving.

SEAFOOD SALAD BOWL

Serves 4
175 g (6 oz) long grain rice
5 ml (1 level tsp) ground turmeric
225 g (8 oz) fresh haddock fillet
1 slice of onion
1 carrot, peeled and sliced
1 bay leaf
1 small green pepper, seeded and diced
170-ml (6-fl oz) jar mussels
2 caps canned pimento, diced
50 g (2 oz) celery, sliced
12 black olives, halved and stoned
125 g (4 oz) peeled prawns
45 ml (3 tbsp) vegetable oil
15 ml (1 tbsp) lemon juice
1 garlic clove, skinned and crushed
salt and freshly ground pepper

Cook the rice in about 1.7 litres (3 pints) boiling salted water with the turmeric added. Drain well and cool.

Place the haddock, onion slice, carrot and bay leaf in a pan with enough salted water to cover. Poach gently for about 10 minutes until tender. Drain the fish and flake the flesh into fork-sized pieces, discarding the skin.

Blanch the green pepper in boiling water for 2 minutes, then drain. Drain the mussels and mix with the rice, pepper, pimento, celery and olives. Stir in the haddock and prawns.

Place the oil, lemon juice, garlic and seasoning in a bowl or screw-topped jar and whisk or shake well together. Pour over the salad and stir to mix. Cover and chill in the refrigerator before serving.

TWO-CHEESE EGG SALAD

Serves 6
125 g (4 oz) shelled hazelnuts
6 eggs, hard-boiled
75 g (3 oz) Danish Blue cheese
75 g (3 oz) full fat soft cheese
100 ml (4 fl oz) single cream
salt and freshly ground pepper
227-g (8-oz) can pineapple chunks
175 g (6 oz) long grain rice, cooked
15 ml (1 tbsp) white wine vinegar
a small bunch watercress

Toast the nuts in a hot oven or under the grill for 5–10 minutes, or until the skins are loose and the kernels brown. Wrap the nuts in a dry tea towel and rub off the skins. Leave to cool, then finely chop 25 g (1 oz) of the nuts.

Shell the eggs and halve them lengthways. Scoop out the yolks and press them through a sieve into a bowl. Place the egg whites in a bowl of cold water until required. Add the Danish Blue and full fat soft cheese, the chopped nuts, cream and seasoning to the egg yolks and beat until well mixed.

Drain the pineapple, reserving 60 ml (4 tbsp) juice. Combine the rice with the pineapple pieces and reserved juice. Stir in the vinegar with the whole hazelnuts, reserving twelve for garnish. Season to taste. Spoon the rice salad into the centre of a serving dish and put watercress sprigs around the edge.

Drain the egg whites and pat them dry with absorbent kitchen paper. Spoon the egg and cheese mixture into a piping bag fitted with a 1-cm ($\frac{1}{2}$-inch) plain nozzle and pipe the mixture into the centres of the egg whites. Sit the eggs on the watercress and top each with a whole hazelnut.

CRUNCHY CHICORY AND CHEESE SALAD

Serves 6
2 large heads chicory
175 g (6 oz) Gruyère cheese
175 g (6 oz) Cotswold or Cheddar cheese
1 green pepper, seeded and chopped
1 head celery, trimmed and chopped
100 g (4 oz) radishes, trimmed and sliced
150 ml ($\frac{1}{4}$ pint) garlic dressing (see page 104)
100 g (4 oz) salted peanuts

Trim and wash the chicory and chop coarsely. Cut the cheese into cubes and place in a salad bowl with the chicory. Add the pepper, celery and radishes and toss together. Pour over the dressing, toss well and sprinkle over the peanuts. Serve accompanied by Hot mustard rolls (see page 117).

ORIENTAL CHICKEN SALAD

Serves 6
1.4-kg (3-lb) oven-ready chicken
1 small onion, skinned and sliced
1 carrot, peeled and sliced
1 bay leaf
6 peppercorns
salt and freshly ground pepper
300 ml ($\frac{1}{2}$ pint) natural yoghurt
5 ml (1 level tsp) paprika
5 ml (1 level tsp) ground coriander
1 large garlic clove, skinned and crushed
30 ml (2 tbsp) lemon juice
1 red pepper, halved, seeded and sliced
225 g (8 oz) bean sprouts, washed
125 g (4 oz) stoned dates, halved
fresh coriander to garnish

Place the chicken in a large saucepan with the onion, carrot, bay leaf and peppercorns. Add water to just cover and cook for about 50 minutes until the chicken is tender. Remove the chicken from the pan and take the meat off the bones. Discard skin and bones and finely shred the meat.

Place the yoghurt, spices, garlic and lemon juice in a bowl, stir to mix, then stir in the still-warm chicken. Season to taste, then leave to cool.

Stir the pepper, bean sprouts and dates into the cool chicken mixture. Cover and chill well in the refrigerator before serving garnished with fresh coriander leaves.

SALAD KEBABS

Satay sticks—fine wooden skewers—are more attractive than metal skewers for this dish.

Serves 4
116-g (4-oz) packet sliced shoulder of ham
4 small tomatoes
5-cm (2-inch) piece cucumber
8 silverskin cocktail onions
pitta bread to serve

Slice the ham into 1-cm ($\frac{1}{2}$-inch) strips. Cut each tomato into eight wedges. Slice the cucumber into four 1-cm ($\frac{1}{2}$-inch) rings, then cut each ring again into four wedges.

Thread alternate pieces of tomato and cucumber on to eight wooden satay sticks, lacing the ham strips in between. Finish each stick with an onion.

To serve salad kebabs, cut pockets in pieces of pitta bread and thickly butter the insides. Plunge the kebabs into the pockets and gently ease away the sticks.

CURRIED PASTA SALAD

Serves 2
$\frac{1}{2}$ small onion, skinned and very finely chopped
30 ml (2 tbsp) dry Vermouth
2 large cooked sausages, thinly sliced
75 g (3 oz) pasta shapes, cooked
75 ml (5 level tbsp) mayonnaise (see page 102)
5 ml (1 level tsp) mild curry paste
5 ml (1 level tsp) apricot jam
5 ml (1 tsp) lemon juice
1 tomato, sliced and black olives to garnish

Place the onion in a saucepan with the Vermouth and boil gently for 2–3 minutes to soften the onion. Leave to cool. Mix the sausages and pasta together in a serving bowl.

Mix together the onion, mayonnaise, curry paste, apricot jam and lemon juice. Pour over the pasta and toss to coat evenly. Serve garnished with slices of tomato and black olives.

CHICKEN IN CRANBERRY MAYONNAISE

Serves 4
1.4-kg (3-lb) oven-ready chicken, poached
125 g (4 oz) fresh cranberries
30 ml (2 level tbsp) granulated sugar
90 ml (6 level tbsp) mayonnaise (see page 102)
15 ml (1 tbsp) horseradish sauce
salt and freshly ground pepper
1 eating apple
lemon juice
a few lettuce leaves
watercress to garnish

While the chicken is cooling, place the cranberries in a small saucepan with 75 ml (5 tbsp) water and bring to the boil. Cover and simmer for about 10 minutes until the cranberries soften and pop. Stir in the sugar and leave to cool. Carve the meat from the chicken and cut into bite-sized pieces.

Place the cold cranberry mixture in a bowl and add the mayonnaise, horseradish and plenty of seasoning. Stir well to combine. Just before serving, core and thinly slice the apple and dip the slices in the lemon juice. Place the apple in a lettuce-lined bowl with the chicken and spoon over the cranberry mayonnaise. Garnish with watercress.

PRAWN RICE SALAD

Serves 4–6
50 g (2 oz) butter
1 medium onion, skinned and finely chopped
100 g (4 oz) long grain rice
300 ml ($\frac{1}{2}$ pint) chicken stock
340-g (12-oz) can sweetcorn kernels with peppers, drained
30 ml (2 tbsp) chopped fresh parsley
100 g (4 oz) peeled prawns, chopped
135 ml (9 tbsp) French dressing (see page 100)
paprika to garnish

Melt the butter in a saucepan. Add the onion and fry for about 5 minutes until transparent, then add the rice and cook for 3 minutes until well coloured—this is an important stage. Pour in the stock, reduce the heat and cook gently, stirring, until the rice has absorbed the liquid. Remove the pan from the heat, add the sweetcorn, parsley and prawns and stir to mix.

Pour the French dressing into the pan and fold in. Arrange the salad in a shallow serving dish and sprinkle a lattice pattern of paprika across the top.

TUNA AND CAULIFLOWER SALAD

Serves 2
1 small head cauliflower, trimmed
198-g (7-oz) can tuna fish, drained
150 ml ($\frac{1}{4}$ pint) natural yoghurt
15 ml (1 tbsp) snipped fresh chives
1.25 ml ($\frac{1}{4}$ level tsp) mustard powder
1 small garlic clove, skinned and crushed with 1.25 ml ($\frac{1}{4}$ level tsp) salt
5 ml (1 tsp) lemon juice
freshly ground pepper
1 red eating apple, cored and diced
a few lettuce leaves

Break the cauliflower into tiny florets and blanch in boiling salted water for 2 minutes. Drain and plunge immediately into cold water, then drain again. Flake the tuna fish.

In a bowl, combine the yoghurt, chives, mustard, garlic salt, lemon juice and enough pepper to season well. Combine the cauliflower, tuna and apple, add the yoghurt dressing and toss well together. Divide between two lettuce-lined plates. Serve with buttered Melba toast (see page 114).

CHICKEN WITH TARRAGON MAYONNAISE

When fresh tarragon is not in season, garnish
this salad with slices of lemon.

Serves 6
6 chicken leg joints
2 sticks celery, trimmed and sliced
200 ml (7 fl oz) medium dry white wine
30 ml (2 tbsp) fresh chopped tarragon or 10 ml (2 level tsp) dried
salt and freshly ground pepper
300 ml ($\frac{1}{2}$ pint) lemon mayonnaise (see page 102–3)
fresh tarragon sprigs to garnish

Skin the chicken joints and divide each one into a leg and thigh portion.
Trim away any fat. Place the joints in a shallow, ovenproof dish into which
they will just fit snugly. Scatter the celery over the chicken. Mix the wine,
herbs and seasoning together and pour over the chicken. Cover the dish and
leave to marinate in a cool place for at least 8 hours, turning once.

Cook the chicken in the marinade, covered, in the oven at 180°C (350°F)
mark 4 for about $1\frac{1}{4}$ hours, or until the chicken is very tender. Remove the
dish from the oven but leave the chicken to cool in the marinade, covered.
When cool, strain off the cooking juices into a saucepan and boil down until
only about 90 ml (6 tbsp) remain. Leave to cool. Ease the bones out of the
chicken pieces and arrange the chicken on a serving plate. Just before serving,
stir the reduced marinade into the mayonnaise and spoon over the chicken.
Garnish with fresh tarragon sprigs, if available.

TURKEY, PINEAPPLE AND PASTA SALAD

Serves 6
700 g ($1\frac{1}{2}$ lb) cold cooked turkey
45 ml (3 tbsp) salad oil
30 ml (2 tbsp) lemon juice
paprika
salt and freshly ground pepper
225 g (8 oz) wholewheat short cut macaroni
two 142-ml (5-fl oz) cartons soured cream
30 ml (2 level tbsp) horseradish sauce
30 ml (2 level tbsp) tomato ketchup
225 g (8 oz) celery, trimmed and sliced
340-g (12-oz) can pineapple cubes, drained
a few lettuce leaves
25 g (1 oz) peanuts to garnish

Cut the turkey into fork-sized pieces. Place the oil, lemon juice, 2.5 ml ($\frac{1}{2}$ level tsp) paprika and seasoning in a bowl and whisk well together. Stir in the turkey and leave in a cool place for about 1 hour. Cook the macaroni in boiling salted water as directed on the packet, then drain well.

In a large bowl, stir together the soured cream, horseradish and ketchup. Fold in the macaroni, celery and pineapple and season well. Stir the turkey into the macaroni mixture, cover and chill well in the refrigerator. Adjust the seasoning. Arrange the salad on a large platter lined with lettuce leaves, garnish with peanuts and sprinkle over a little more paprika.

CHICKEN AND GRAPE SALAD

Serves 4–6
1.4-kg (3-lb) roasting chicken
1 small onion, skinned and sliced
1 carrot, peeled and sliced
1 bay leaf
6 peppercorns
2 eggs
90 ml (6 tbsp) lemon juice (about 2 lemons)
45 ml (3 tbsp) thin honey
150 ml ($\frac{1}{4}$ pint) whipping cream
225 g (8 oz) white grapes, halved and seeded
50 g (2 oz) seedless raisins
salt and freshly ground pepper
lettuce and paprika to garnish

Place the chicken in a large saucepan with the onion, carrot, bay leaf and peppercorns. Add enough water to just cover and cook for about 50 minutes, until the chicken is tender. Leave the chicken to cool in the stock, then remove the chicken from the pan, take the meat off the bones and divide the meat into bite-sized pieces.

Beat the eggs with 60 ml (4 tbsp) lemon juice and the honey. Cook gently in a double saucepan, or in a bowl over a pan of water, until thick, then turn into a large bowl, cover the surface with damp greaseproof paper and leave to cool.

Whip the cream lightly, then fold it into the cold egg and lemon mixture. Add the grapes, the remaining lemon juice, the chicken, raisins and seasonings to the sauce and mix well together.

Serve garnished with lettuce and paprika, and accompanied by cold cooked rice.

CHICKEN À LA GRECQUE

Illustrated in colour facing page 64

Serves 4
25 g (1 oz) butter, softened
1.4-kg (3-lb) oven-ready chicken
200 ml (7 fl oz) chicken stock
75 ml (5 tbsp) vegetable oil
15 ml (1 tbsp) white wine vinegar
10 ml (2 level tsp) tomato purée
1 large garlic clove, skinned and crushed
7.5 ml (1½ level tsp) chopped fresh thyme or basil or 2.5 ml (½ level tsp) dried
salt and freshly ground pepper
175 g (6 oz) small button onions, skinned
5 ml (1 level tsp) caster sugar
225 g (8 oz) button mushrooms, wiped and halved
lettuce, green pepper and watercress to serve

Preheat the oven to 200°C (400°F) mark 6. Spread the butter over the chicken. Place in a small roasting tin with the stock and roast in the oven for about 1½ hours, basting frequently, until tender.

Meanwhile, place 45 ml (3 tbsp) oil, the vinegar, tomato purée, garlic, herbs and seasoning in a bowl or screw-topped jar and whisk or shake well together. Blanch the onions in boiling water for 5 minutes, then drain well. Heat the remaining oil in a frying pan, add the sugar and onions and cook for 2 minutes, add the mushrooms and toss over a high heat for a few seconds. Tip the contents of the frying pan into the dressing.

Joint the hot chicken into eight pieces, arrange on a serving plate and spoon the vegetables and dressing over it. Chill well in the refrigerator.

Serve with crisp lettuce, sliced green pepper and watercress.

MACARONI SALAD LUNCH

Serves 2
125 g (4 oz) wholewheat short cut macaroni
30 ml (2 tbsp) corn oil
30 ml (2 level tbsp) sweet pickle
1 orange
100 g (4 oz) Cheshire cheese
5-cm (2-inch) piece cucumber
2 sticks tender celery, trimmed and finely sliced
salt and freshly ground pepper
6 small spring onions, trimmed and chopped
plain potato crisps or garlic croûtons (see page 117) to serve

Cook the macaroni in boiling salted water for about 12 minutes until tender, then drain well. Put the oil and pickle into a large bowl. Finely grate in the orange rind and whisk together. Add the pasta and fold in until evenly coated with dressing.

Holding the orange over the bowl, use a serrated knife to remove all traces of pith, then remove the fruit segments from the membrane and add them to the bowl. Dice the cheese and cucumber and fold them into the pasta with the celery. Season well with salt and pepper. Chill lightly in the refrigerator, then scatter with chopped onion just before serving. Serve with a bowl of plain potato crisps or garlic croûtons to scatter on each helping.

RED BEAN AND CHICKEN SALAD

Serves 6
45 ml (3 tbsp) white wine vinegar
90 ml (6 tbsp) olive oil
2.5 ml ($\frac{1}{2}$ level tsp) dried sage
salt and freshly ground pepper
225 g (8 oz) red kidney beans, soaked overnight
1.1-kg ($2\frac{1}{2}$-lb) roasting chicken (oven-ready weight)
2 chicken stock cubes
1.1 litre (2 pints) boiling water
1 bay leaf
100 g (4 oz) spring onions, trimmed and chopped
198-g (7-oz) can corn niblets, drained

Place the vinegar, oil, sage and seasoning in a bowl or screw-topped jar and whisk or shake well together. Leave to infuse while the beans and chicken are cooking.

Drain the beans and place them in a deep saucepan with the whole chicken. Crumble in the stock cubes and add the water to the pan with the bay leaf, 15 ml (1 level tbsp) salt and pepper. Cover, bring to the boil and boil for 10 minutes, then reduce the heat and simmer for about 1 hour, or until both chicken and beans are tender. Alternatively cook in a pressure cooker at HIGH (15 lb) pressure for about 20 minutes.

Drain and cool the chicken and beans. Carve off all the meat from the carcass, discarding the skin and bones, and chop the meat roughly.

Combine the chicken with the spring onions and combine the beans and corn. Pile the chicken in the centre of a dish and arrange the bean mixture round it. Whisk or shake the dressing once more before pouring it over the salad. Chill in the refrigerator before serving.

MOULDED KIPPER AND EGG RING

Illustrated in colour facing page 48

Serves 8
170-g (6-oz) pack boil-in-the-bag kipper fillets
8 eggs
150 ml ($\frac{1}{4}$ pint) liquid aspic
40 g ($1\frac{1}{2}$ oz) butter
40 g ($1\frac{1}{2}$ oz) plain flour
450 ml ($\frac{3}{4}$ pint) milk
5 ml (1 tsp) anchovy essence
142-ml (5-fl oz) carton soured cream
salt and freshly ground pepper
paprika
30 ml (2 level tbsp) powdered gelatine
For the salad
450 g (1 lb) French beans, trimmed and halved
450 g (1 lb) green apples
50 g (2 oz) shelled walnuts, roughly chopped
135 ml (9 tbsp) French dressing (see page 100)

Cook the kippers as directed on the packet. Remove from the bag and flake, reserving the juices, and leave to cool. Hard-boil seven of the eggs, cool, shell and roughly chop. Separate the remaining egg. Stir one chopped egg into the aspic, pour into the base of a 1.3-litre ($2\frac{1}{4}$-pint) ring mould, and chill to set.

Melt the butter in a saucepan, stir in the flour and cook for 1 minute. Remove from the heat and gradually add the milk, stirring all the time. Stir in the reserved kipper juices. Return to the heat and cook for 2–3 minutes, stirring, until thickened. Remove from the heat and beat in the egg yolk from the uncooked egg. Leave to cool. When cool, add the anchovy essence and soured cream, season to taste with salt, pepper and paprika, then add the flaked fish and remaining chopped eggs.

Sprinkle the gelatine into 120 ml (8 tbsp) water in a small bowl. Stand the bowl in a pan of hot water and heat until the gelatine has dissolved. Stir into the mixture. Stiffly whisk the egg white and fold lightly into the mixture, using a metal spoon. Turn into the mould and chill in the refrigerator for 2–3 hours. When set, unmould the ring on to a serving plate.

To make the salad, cook the beans in boiling salted water for 5–10 minutes until tender. Drain and cool. Core and thinly slice the apples. Combine the beans, apple and walnuts. Toss in French dressing until coated and pile into the centre of the kipper and egg ring.

GREEK SALAD

Olive oil and Feta cheese are both essential
ingredients of this salad. Feta cheese is available from many delicatessen shops.

Serves 4
2 large beef tomatoes
1 green pepper
½ medium cucumber
50 g (2 oz) black or stuffed olives
225 g (8 oz) Feta cheese
120 ml (8 tbsp) olive oil
30–45 ml (2–3 tbsp) lemon juice
salt and freshly ground pepper

Cut the tomatoes into eighths. Halve, seed and slice the pepper thinly and slice the cucumber thickly. Stone the black olives, if used. Arrange the tomatoes, pepper, cucumber and olives in a salad bowl. Dice the cheese and add to the bowl, reserving a few dice for garnish. Pour over the olive oil, followed by the lemon juice and season well. Toss the salad well together. Crumble over the remaining cheese cubes and serve with pitta bread.

SALMON RICE

Serves 4
50-g (1¾-oz) can anchovies
milk
225 g (8 oz) long grain rice
75 ml (5 tbsp) French dressing (see page 100)
1 medium onion, skinned and finely chopped
30 ml (2 tbsp) chopped fresh parsley
213-g (7½-oz) can pink salmon, drained
2 eggs, hard-boiled
1 small avocado

Drain and separate the anchovies and place them in a bowl. Cover them with milk and leave for 30 minutes. Meanwhile, cook the rice in boiling salted water for about 10 minutes until tender. Rinse in cold water to cool quickly, then drain well and place in a bowl.

Drain the anchovies and chop them. Pour the French dressing over the rice, add the onion, parsley and anchovies and mix well. Flake the salmon, discarding the dark skin and bone. Lightly fold it into the rice, being careful not to break the salmon down too finely.

To serve, arrange the salad on a shallow serving dish. Shell and slice the eggs. Halve, stone, peel and slice the avocado and dip the slices in lemon juice to prevent discoloration. Arrange the egg and avocado slices over the rice mixture.

INSALATA DI FRUTTI DI MARE (SEAFOOD SALAD)

A salad reminiscent of the Mediterranean with many different kinds of seafood marinated in an oil and garlic dressing.

Serves 4
350 g (12 oz) squid
750 g (1½ lb) fresh mussels
125 g (4 oz) prawns, cooked and peeled
30 ml (2 tbsp) distilled malt vinegar
6 scallops, shelled
225 g (8 oz) crabmeat, cooked and flaked
150 ml (¼ pint) olive oil
1 garlic clove, skinned and crushed
30 ml (2 tbsp) lemon juice
salt and freshly ground pepper

Prepare the squid by pulling the head and tentacles from the body and discarding the black ink sac and 'quill' from the tail piece. Remove any scaly film and wash well. Cut into thin rings.

Scrub the mussels, discarding any which are open. Put them in a frying pan and cover. Cook on a high heat for about 5 minutes or until the shells open. Cool a little, then lift the meat from the shells and put it in a bowl. Add the prawns.

In a saucepan, boil about 1.7 litres (3 pints) water with the vinegar. Add the scallops and squid and cook for 4 minutes. Drain, cool and cut the scallops into several pieces. Add to the bowl with the crabmeat. Pour over the olive oil, garlic and lemon juice and season with salt and pepper. Marinate for a few hours before serving. Serve accompanied by hot garlic bread (see page 114) and an onion and tomato salad (see page 33).

BUFFET-STYLE HAM AND TONGUE SLAW

Illustrated in colour facing page 64

Serves 6
two 113-g (4-oz) packets sliced Old Smokey ham
two 113-g (4-oz) packets sliced cooked tongue
175 g (6 oz) radishes
2 eating apples
450 g (1 lb) crisp cabbage heart or white cabbage, finely shredded
150 ml (¼ pint) mayonnaise (see page 102)
45 ml (3 level tbsp) chopped fresh mint
salt and freshly ground pepper

Using kitchen scissors, cut the ham and tongue into thin strips about 6.5 cm (2½ inches) long. Top and tail the radishes. Leave a few whole and thinly slice the remainder. Polish the apples with a clean dry cloth, then quarter, core and thinly slice them.

Mix the meats, cabbage, sliced radishes, apples, mayonnaise and mint well together and season generously. Cover the dish and chill in the refrigerator for several hours to allow the flavours to mingle. To serve, spoon the salad into a shallow dish and garnish with the whole radishes.

CORONATION CHICKEN

This recipe was created by the Cordon Bleu school in London the year Queen Elizabeth was crowned—hence its name.

Serves 8
2.3-kg (5-lb) cold cooked chicken
15 ml (1 tbsp) vegetable oil
1 small onion, skinned and finely chopped
15 ml (1 level tbsp) curry paste
15 ml (1 tbsp) tomato purée
100 ml (4 fl oz) red wine
1 bay leaf
juice of ½ lemon
4 canned apricot halves, finely chopped
300 ml (½ pint) mayonnaise (see page 102)
100 ml (4 fl oz) whipping cream
salt and freshly ground pepper
watercress to garnish

Remove all the meat from the chicken and dice. In a small pan, heat the oil, add the onion and cook for about 3 minutes, or until softened. Add the curry paste, tomato purée, wine, bay leaf and lemon juice. Simmer, uncovered, for about 10 minutes until well reduced. Strain and leave to cool.

Press the chopped apricot through a sieve to produce a purée. Beat the cooled sauce into the mayonnaise with the apricot purée. Lightly whip the cream and fold into the mixture. Season, adding a little extra lemon juice if necessary. Toss the chicken pieces into the sauce and transfer to a serving dish. Garnish with watercress and serve with rice salad and a cucumber side salad, if liked.

SALADE NIÇOISE

Serves 4
198-g (7-oz) can tuna fish, drained
225 g (8 oz) tomatoes, skinned and quartered
50 g (2 oz) black olives, stoned
$\frac{1}{2}$ small cucumber, thinly sliced
225 g (8 oz) cooked French beans
2 eggs, hard-boiled, shelled and quartered
15 ml (1 tbsp) chopped fresh parsley
15 ml (1 tbsp) chopped fresh basil
150 ml ($\frac{1}{4}$ pint) garlic French dressing (see page 101)
8 anchovies, halved

F lake the tuna into fairly large chunks. Arrange in a salad bowl with the tomatoes, olives, cucumber, beans and egg quarters. Add the parsley and basil to the French dressing, mix well and pour over the salad. Arrange the anchovy fillets in a lattice pattern over the salad and allow to stand for 30 minutes before serving. Serve with crusty French bread.

CHICKEN SALAD WITH RICE

Serves 4–6
100 g (4 oz) long grain rice
150 ml ($\frac{1}{4}$ pint) French dressing (see page 100)
550 g ($1\frac{1}{4}$ lb) cauliflower, trimmed
450 g (1 lb) cold cooked chicken
$\frac{1}{2}$ green pepper, seeded
2 red eating apples
juice of 1 lemon
142-ml (5-fl oz) carton soured cream

C ook the rice in boiled salted water for 10–15 minutes until tender. When cooked, drain the rice, transfer it to a bowl and pour over half the French dressing. Stir, then leave until cold.

Break the cauliflower into tiny florets, then plunge it into boiling water for 1 minute. Drain, then plunge the cauliflower into cold water and drain again. Cut the chicken and pepper into strips. Core and dice the apples and dip in the lemon juice to prevent discoloration.

In a bowl, combine the cauliflower, pepper and apples. Whisk or shake the remaining dressing, pour it over and spoon through. Reserve 30–45 ml (2–3 tbsp) of the mixture for garnish.

Fold the soured cream, chicken and rice into the cauliflower mixture. Pile the salad into a bowl and top with the reserved cauliflower, peppers and apple.

Clockwise from top: Chicken à la Grecque (*page 58*); Buffet-style ham and tongue slaw (*page 62*) and Brawn and cottage cheese rolls (*page 72*).

Salmagundy (*recipe opposite*).

SALMAGUNDY
Illustrated in colour opposite

This is an elaborate old English dish made from various cold meats, layered up with salt herrings, pickled vegetables and salad ingredients. The finished dish can be as high as 60 cm (2 feet) but below is a simpler version, suitable for a grand summer dinner party.

Serves 8
2.5-kg (5-lb) oven-ready duckling
salt and freshly ground pepper
2-kg (4-lb) oven-ready chicken
25 g (1 oz) butter, melted
450 g (1 lb) carrots, peeled
450 g (1 lb) potatoes, peeled
4 sticks celery, trimmed
225 g (8 oz) tomatoes, skinned
1 cucumber, peeled
450 g (1 lb) peas, cooked
300 ml ($\frac{1}{2}$ pint) French dressing (see page 100)
4 eggs, hard-boiled (optional)
mayonnaise (optional)
radishes, gherkins and parsley sprigs to garnish

Preheat the oven to 200°C (400°F) mark 6. Sprinkle the duck liberally with salt and place on a rack or trivet in a roasting tin. Roast in the top of the oven for about 2 hours or until the juices run clear. Cool.

Brush the chicken with melted butter and sprinkle with salt and pepper. Place in a shallow roasting tin and roast on the lowest shelf of the oven for about $1\frac{1}{2}$ hours or until golden brown and the juices run clear. Cool.

Remove the skin from both chicken and duck and remove all the flesh from the bones. Cut the flesh into thin slices. Cut the carrots into 0.5-cm ($\frac{1}{4}$-inch) wide long strips and cook in boiling salted water for 8–10 minutes, or until tender. Drain. Cook the potatoes in boiling salted water for 15 minutes until tender, drain and dice finely. Thinly slice the celery, tomatoes and cucumber.

Choose a large oval platter for layering up the salmagundy. Place potato dice and peas in the bottom of the dish to give a flat base. Arrange carrot strips around the dish (not quite to the edge) following the oval pattern. Pour over a little French dressing. Next, arrange a layer of cucumber, slightly inside the carrot layer so that the carrots may be seen. Top with more layers of chicken meat, peas, tomato slices, celery, duck meat, etc, until all the ingredients are used. Remember to make each layer inside the one below so that the lower layers may all be seen. Dress each layer with French dressing. Garnish the upper layer with parsley sprigs if wished.

Halve the eggs and top each half with a little mayonnaise if used. Garnish with a few radish slices and parsley sprigs. Make the gherkins into fans and arrange alternately with the eggs around the edge of the dish. Sliced radishes may be pushed into the layers of the salmagundy to give extra colour.

SAUSAGE AND BEAN SALAD

Illustrated in colour facing page 49

Serves 4
125 g (4 oz) large shell pasta
700 g (1½ lb) broad beans, podded
225-g (8-oz) piece French garlic sausage
213-g (7½-oz) can red kidney beans, drained
For the dressing
45 ml (3 tbsp) vegetable oil
10 ml (2 tsp) wine vinegar
grated rind and juice of 1 orange
45 ml (3 tbsp) chopped fresh parsley
salt and freshly ground black pepper

Cook the pasta in boiling salted water for about 10 minutes, or until tender. Drain, cool under cold running water and drain again. Cook the broad beans in boiling salted water for about 15 minutes, then drain and leave to cool. Slip off the outer skins. Cut the garlic sausage into small chunks.

Place the oil, vinegar, orange rind and 45 ml (3 tbsp) orange juice, the parsley and plenty of seasoning in a bowl or screw-topped jar and whisk or shake well together.

Place the pasta, broad beans, sausage and red kidney beans in a serving bowl, pour over the dressing and toss together. Cover and chill in the refrigerator before serving.

CURRIED RICE SALAD

Serves 2
50 g (2 oz) long grain rice
60 ml (4 level tbsp) mayonnaise (see page 102)
2.5–5 ml (½–1 level tsp) curry paste
a little grated orange rind
freshly ground pepper
2 canned pineapple rings
100 g (4 oz) sliced ham
chopped fresh parsley to garnish

Cook the rice in boiling salted water for about 10 minutes, until tender but not mushy. Drain and rinse with cold water to cool quickly. Drain well.

In a bowl, combine the mayonnaise, curry paste, orange rind and freshly ground pepper to taste. With a sharp knife or scissors, cut the pineapple into small pieces and fold into half the mayonnaise mixture with the rice.

Arrange the rice in a bed on a flat serving dish. Cut the ham into julienne strips and fold into the remaining curried mayonnaise. Pile on top of the rice and garnish with chopped parsley.

BACON, APPLE AND CELERY SALAD

Serves 4
450-g (1-lb) boil-in-the-bag bacon joint
2 sticks celery, trimmed and sliced
150 ml ($\frac{1}{4}$ pint) natural yoghurt
2.5 ml ($\frac{1}{2}$ level tsp) hot curry powder
15 ml (1 tbsp) mango chutney
salt and freshly ground pepper
2 medium eating apples
50 g (2 oz) seedless raisins
a few lettuce leaves (optional)

Cook the bacon joint according to packet instructions, cool and slice into strips. Place in a bowl and combine with the celery.

Place the yoghurt, curry powder, chutney and seasoning in a bowl and whisk together. Peel, core and slice the apples and stir into the dressing to prevent discoloration.

Add the apple and dressing to the ham and celery with the raisins and mix well. Cover and chill in the refrigerator for several hours.

To serve, stir the salad and transfer to a serving bowl or individual lettuce-lined plates. If liked, serve with Cheese straws (see page 119).

HAWAIIAN PINEAPPLE CHICKEN

Serves 4
1.4-kg (3-lb) chicken, cooked
1 large pineapple (about 1.4 kg/3 lb)
2 sticks celery, trimmed
75 g (3 oz) walnut halves, broken
200 ml (7 fl oz) mayonnaise
45 ml (3 tbsp) single cream
lemon juice
salt and freshly ground pepper

Remove the flesh from the chicken and dice. Cut the pineapple lengthways into quarters, keeping the green top on if possible. Cut out all the flesh and chop, discarding the hard core. Add it to the chicken in a large bowl. Finely slice the celery and add it to the bowl with the walnuts, reserving a few walnut halves for garnish. Toss the salad well.

Put the mayonnaise and cream in a bowl, add a little lemon juice and season to taste. Add to the chicken mixture and toss well. Put the pineapple quarter shells on a flat serving dish and divide the chicken mixture between them, piling it high. Garnish with the reserved walnut halves.

CURRIED POTATO AND FRANKFURTER SALAD

Serves 6
900 g (2 lb) new potatoes, scraped
two 213-g (7½-oz) packets frankfurters
10 ml (2 tsp) lemon juice
30 ml (2 tbsp) wine vinegar
10–15 ml (2–3 level tsp) curry paste
300 ml (½ pint) mayonnaise (see page 102)
50 g (2 oz) gherkins, chopped
25 g (1 oz) silverskin cocktail onions, finely chopped
chopped fresh parsley to garnish

Cut the potatoes into large dice. Cook in boiling salted water for 8–10 minutes until just cooked but still firm. Drain, transfer to a bowl and leave to cool.

Cook the frankfurters in fast-boiling water for 5 minutes. Drain and cool. Slice each sausage into four pieces. Chop the end pieces and add them to the potatoes.

Stir the lemon juice, vinegar and curry paste into the mayonnaise, then lightly fold the curried mayonnaise, gherkins and onions into the potatoes and sausages. Pile on to a large flat serving plate. Garnish with the remaining pieces of frankfurter and sprinkle with parsley.

ITALIAN TOMATO AND EGG SALAD

Serves 6
6 eggs, hard-boiled
6 medium tomatoes, skinned
49-g (1¾-oz) can anchovies
50 g (2 oz) stuffed olives
10 ml (2 level tsp) tomato purée
150 ml (¼ pint) French dressing (see page 100)
chopped fresh parsley to garnish

Shell and slice the hard-boiled eggs and arrange on an oval platter. Halve the tomatoes and lay them on top of the egg slices. Halve each anchovy and lay two pieces across each tomato to make a cross. Slice the olives and use to garnish each tomato half. Sprinkle the rest over the egg. Add the tomato purée to the French dressing, whisk or shake together, then spoon over the salad. Garnish with a little parsley. Serve with Cheese bread (see page 113).

RUSSIAN SALAD

Serves 4
1 small cauliflower, trimmed
125 g (4 oz) turnips, peeled
125 g (4 oz) carrots, peeled
225 g (8 oz) potatoes, peeled
1 small cooked beetroot, skinned
2 medium tomatoes, skinned
salt and freshly ground pepper
150 ml ($\frac{1}{4}$ pint) mayonnaise (see page 102)
lemon juice
125 g (4 oz) tongue, diced
125 g (4 oz) prawns, peeled
125 g (4 oz) peas, cooked
4 gherkins, chopped
30 ml (2 tbsp) capers
6 olives
6 anchovies

Break the cauliflower into small florets and cook in boiling salted water for about 8 minutes until tender. Drain, rinse in cold water and drain again. Dice the turnips, carrots and potatoes finely and cook, rinse and drain as above. Dice the beetroot and tomatoes, discarding the seeds.

Place a layer of cauliflower in a deep salad bowl and season well. Thin the mayonnaise with a little lemon juice and spread a little over the cauliflower. Layer the turnips, carrots, potatoes, peas, beetroot, tomatoes, tongue and prawns in the same way, ending with a layer of mayonnaise. Sprinkle over the gherkins and capers and garnish with the olives and anchovies. Serve with wholemeal bread.

FRESH SARDINES WITH HERBS

Serves 4
900 g (2 lb) fresh sardines (at least 12)
60 ml (4 tbsp) finely chopped fresh mint
60 ml (4 tbsp) finely chopped fresh parsley
60 ml (4 tbsp) finely chopped fresh sage
grated rind of 2 lemons
120 ml (8 tbsp) lemon juice
300 ml ($\frac{1}{2}$ pint) salad oil
2 medium onions, skinned and finely sliced
salt and freshly ground pepper
lemon wedges to garnish

Wash the sardines well and gut if preferred. Reserving 15 ml (1 tbsp) mixed herbs to garnish, mix the remainder with the lemon rind, juice, oil, onion and seasoning.

Grill the sardines for 5–7 minutes on each side, basting with the herb dressing. Leave in the dressing to cool completely. Sprinkle with the reserved herbs before serving. Garnish with lemon wedges.

AMERICAN CHEF'S SALAD

This main meal salad consists of vegetables arranged in a bowl with some form of protein food, such as meat, cheese or egg. It should be tossed at the table after the guests have seen it—choosing either a vinaigrette or Blue cheese dressing.

Serves 4
225 g (8 oz) ham
225 g (8 oz) cold cooked chicken
225 g (8 oz) Emmenthal cheese
1 iceberg lettuce
2 eggs, hard-boiled, shelled and quartered
6 cherry tomatoes, halved or 2 tomatoes, quartered
3 spring onions, trimmed and finely chopped
150 ml ($\frac{1}{4}$ pint) French dressing (see page 100) or Blue cheese dressing (see page 110)

Cut the ham and chicken into fine strips and dice the cheese. Wash the lettuce and shred finely. Place in an oval dish. Arrange the meat and cheese alternately around the edge of the dish. Place the tomatoes and egg in the centre of the dish. Sprinkle over the spring onions and serve the dressing separately.

SIDE SALADS

The choice of a side salad obviously depends on the food it has to accompany. Probably the most popular side salad is a simple green salad of crisp lettuce leaves, cucumber, green pepper and cress, dressed with a plain French dressing. This will go well with almost any dish and is delicious served with steak or a pizza.

There are numerous side salads to choose from, however. Some are more elaborate than others. Obviously, a rich dish needs only a very simple salad to accompany it.

Side salads should be attractively presented on individual salad plates or in small salad bowls. It is best to dress a salad in a large bowl and then spoon it into the individual bowls after tossing well. More than one side salad may be served if they are very simple, comprising only one or two ingredients each.

BRAWN AND COTTAGE CHEESE ROLLS

Illustrated in colour facing page 64

Serves 4
1 medium cucumber
175 g (6 oz) cottage cheese
salt and freshly ground pepper
two 100-g (3½-oz) packets sliced brawn (Hungarian Style)
450 g (1 lb) firm ripe tomatoes
45 ml (3 tbsp) vegetable oil
15 ml (1 tbsp) white wine vinegar
5 ml (1 level tsp) tomato purée

Peel the cucumber, reserving about one third of the skin. Cut half the cucumber into fine dice and the remainder into fine strips. Shred the reserved skin. Beat the dice into the cottage cheese with seasoning to taste. Divide the cheese mixture between the slices of brawn and roll up. Cover and chill for about 30 minutes. Place side by side on a flat serving dish.

Skin and quarter the tomatoes, remove the seeds and shred the flesh. Place in a bowl with the remaining cucumber. Place the oil, vinegar, tomato purée and seasoning in a bowl or screw-topped jar and whisk or shake well together. Pour over the cucumber and tomatoes. Toss together. Just before serving, pile the salad round the rolls and garnish with the shredded cucumber skin.

LOBSTER MAYONNAISE

Serves 2
1 medium lobster, cooked
1 lettuce
150 ml (¼ pint) mayonnaise (see page 102)
1 egg, hard-boiled, shelled and sliced

Twist the claws and pinchers off the cooked lobster. Using a hammer crack open the large claws and carefully extract the meat. Remove the thin membrane from the centre of each claw. Cut off the head. Split the lobster right down the middle of the body from the head to tail, using a strong pointed knife. Open out and remove the gills, the dark intestinal vein which runs down the tail, and the small stomach sac which lies in the head. Extract the meat from the lobster, reserving the flesh from the claws and any coral roe for garnishing. Flake the remaining flesh with a fork or divide it into neat pieces.

Shred some of the outer leaves of the lettuce and arrange in a salad bowl. Mix the lobster meat with the mayonnaise and pile lightly on top of the lettuce. Top with slices of egg, the lettuce heart, divided into quarters, the claw meat of the lobster and any coral.

SMOKED SAUSAGE AND CHEESE SALAD

Serves 6–8
450 g (1 lb) smoked pork sausage
350 g (12 oz) Gouda cheese
1 medium onion, skinned and chopped
60 ml (4 tbsp) chopped fresh parsley
90 ml (6 tbsp) French dressing (see page 100)

Cut the sausage into slices about 0.3 cm ($\frac{1}{8}$ inch) thick. Cut the cheese into 1-cm ($\frac{1}{2}$-inch) cubes. Add the onion and parsley to the dressing and whisk or shake well together. Toss the sausage and cheese in the dressing. Cover and leave for the flavours to infuse for about 1 hour before serving.

MINT AND CUCUMBER FISH SALAD

Serves 4
900 g (2 lb) fresh cod fillet (the thick end is the best choice)
juice of $\frac{1}{2}$ lemon
salt
$\frac{1}{2}$ cucumber, finely diced
30 ml (2 tbsp) chopped fresh mint
30 ml (2 tbsp) chopped fresh parsley
120 ml (8 tbsp) French dressing (see page 100)
For the garnish
25–50 g (1–2 oz) peeled prawns
lemon wedges
mint sprigs

Wash and skin the fish and cut it into three or four pieces. Sprinkle with lemon juice and salt. Place in a pan and add enough cold water to cover. Gently poach for about 10 minutes until tender (the fish should flake easily and look milky white all through). Remove the pan from the heat and leave the fish in the cooking liquid until quite cold.

Flake the fish very coarsely into a large bowl, removing any bones. Add the cucumber, chopped mint and parsley and pour over the French dressing. Toss well together until all the ingredients are combined and coated with dressing. Take care not to break up the natural flakes of fish. Pile the mixture into individual dishes and garnish each one with prawns, a lemon wedge and a sprig of mint. Alternatively, serve in a large salad bowl accompanied by mayonnaise, tossed green salad and French bread.

TOMATO AND COURGETTE SALAD

Serves 6
450 g (1 lb) firm ripe tomatoes
450 g (1 lb) courgettes
45 ml (3 tbsp) vegetable oil
a few sprigs of fresh rosemary
90 ml (6 tbsp) French dressing (see page 100)

Skin and quarter the tomatoes and scoop the centres into a sieve over a bowl. Reserve the juice and discard the seeds. Trim and wipe the courgettes and cut them into 0.5-cm ($\frac{1}{4}$-inch) slices. Heat the oil in a large frying pan and sauté the courgettes until golden brown—don't overcook them as they're best with a hint of crispness. Drain the courgettes and place them in a bowl with the tomatoes.

Strip the rosemary spears from their stems and chop enough to give 10 ml (2 tsp). Add to the French dressing in a bowl or screw-topped jar. Add the reserved tomato juices, whisk or shake well together and pour over the still-warm vegetables. Gently turn to blend, then chill well in the refrigerator. Pile into a salad bowl for serving.

CARROT AND PINEAPPLE SLAW

Serves 2
10 ml (2 tsp) corn oil
10 ml (2 tsp) distilled malt vinegar
10 ml (2 tsp) pineapple juice from can
a pinch of sugar
a dash of mild curry paste
225 g (8 oz) carrots, peeled
2 small canned pineapple rings
30 ml (2 tbsp) sultanas
salt and freshly ground pepper

Place the oil, vinegar, pineapple juice, sugar and curry paste in a bowl and whisk well together. Coarsely grate the carrots into the dressing. Using scissors, snip the pineapple into small pieces and add it to the dressing. Stir in the sultanas. Check the seasoning, cover and refrigerate until needed.

RICE SALAD RING

Serves 8
225 g (8 oz) long grain rice
1 green pepper, seeded and diced
3 caps canned pimento, diced
198-g (7-oz) can corn niblets, drained
75 ml (5 tbsp) chopped fresh parsley
50 g (2 oz) salted peanuts
45 ml (3 tbsp) lemon juice
celery salt
freshly ground black pepper
watercress to garnish

Lightly oil a 1.4-litre (2½-pint) ring mould. Cook the rice in plenty of boiling salted water for 10–15 minutes until tender, then drain. Rinse through with cold water and drain thoroughly. Leave to cool completely. Blanch the pepper in boiling water for 1 minute, drain, rinse in cold water and drain again.

In a large bowl, mix the cold rice, pepper and pimento, corn niblets, parsley, peanuts and lemon juice, and season well with celery salt and pepper. Press the salad into the mould and chill well in the refrigerator. Turn out for serving on to a flat serving plate and fill the centre of the salad ring with watercress.

TABOULEH

Serves 6–8
225 g (8 oz) bulgar wheat
3 spring onions, trimmed
225 g (8 oz) fresh parsley
3 large sprigs mint
60 ml (4 tbsp) olive oil
juice of 2 lemons
salt and freshly ground pepper
a few vine or lettuce leaves
black olives and lemon slices to garnish

Soak the bulgar wheat in plenty of cold water for 30 minutes. Drain well in a sieve, then spread it out on a dry tea towel and leave it to dry.

Finely chop the spring onions. Chop the parsley and mint. (Such a large quantity of parsley can be chopped more easily in several batches in a blender or food processor.) Mix the bulgar wheat, parsley and mint together in a bowl, add the olive oil and lemon juice and season well to taste. Serve the salad on a serving dish lined with vine or lettuce leaves. Garnish with olives and lemon slices. Pitta bread makes an excellent accompaniment to this refreshing Middle Eastern dish.

JELLIED GAZPACHO SALAD

Serves 6
15 g ($\frac{1}{2}$ oz) gelatine
600 ml (1 pint) water
1 chicken stock cube
30 ml (2 tbsp) distilled malt vinegar
2.5 ml ($\frac{1}{2}$ level tsp) salt
5 ml (1 level tsp) paprika
2.5 ml ($\frac{1}{2}$ level tsp) dried basil
a few drops of Tabasco sauce
1 small pepper, seeded and finely diced
1 garlic clove, skinned and crushed (optional)
1 small onion, skinned and finely chopped
50 g (2 oz) celery, trimmed and finely chopped
350 g (12 oz) tomatoes, skinned and chopped

Sprinkle the gelatine into 150 ml ($\frac{1}{4}$ pint) cold water in a bowl. Place the bowl over a pan of hot water and heat gently until the gelatine has dissolved. Remove from the heat.

In another pan, heat the remaining water, add the stock cube and stir until dissolved. Remove from the heat and add the vinegar, salt, paprika, basil, Tabasco and the gelatine liquid. Chill in the refrigerator until of the consistency of unbeaten egg white.

Blanch the pepper in fast-boiling water for 1 minute. Drain and cool. Fold the garlic, if used, the onion, celery, pepper and tomatoes into the setting mixture and pour into a 1.1-litre (2-pint) plain ring mould. Return to the refrigerator until set.

To unmould the salad, dip the mould in hot water, then place a serving plate upside-down over the mould and invert the salad on to the plate. Remove the mould and serve the salad with Soured cream dressing (see page 104).

GREEN BEAN AND TOMATO SALAD

Serves 4
225 g (8 oz) fresh or frozen haricot verts, trimmed
225 g (8 oz) tomatoes, skinned
15 ml (1 tbsp) chopped fresh herbs, such as parsley, thyme, mint or basil
150 ml ($\frac{1}{4}$ pint) French dressing (see page 100)

Place the beans in boiling salted water and cook for 10–15 minutes until just tender. Drain, rinse in cold water and drain again. Slice the tomatoes and pile into a serving dish with the beans. Mix the herbs with the dressing, pour over the salad and toss well before serving.

ORIENTAL SALAD BOWL

Serves 4–6
450 g (1 lb) Chinese cabbage leaves, trimmed and shredded
100 g (4 oz) carrots, peeled and coarsely grated
2 red apples, cored and chopped
425-g (15-oz) can crushed pineapple
1 bunch watercress to garnish
For the dressing
90 ml (6 tbsp) corn oil
30 ml (2 tbsp) distilled malt vinegar
60 ml (4 tbsp) pineapple juice from can
salt and freshly ground pepper
5 ml (1 level tsp) French mustard

In a bowl, combine the Chinese cabbage, carrot and apple. Drain the pineapple, reserving the juice and add the crushed fruit to the Chinese leaves mixture.

Place all the dressing ingredients in a bowl or screw-topped jar and whisk or shake well together. Add to the salad and toss lightly. Pile into a serving bowl and arrange watercress sprigs around the edge.

WINTER SALAD

Serves 4
2 eating apples, cored and chopped
4 sticks celery, trimmed and chopped
1 medium cooked beetroot, skinned and diced
$\frac{1}{2}$ small onion, skinned and finely chopped
mayonnaise or salad cream to bind (see page 102)
a few chopped walnuts (optional)

Mix the apples, celery, beetroot and onion and add sufficient mayonnaise or salad cream to bind together. Pile on to a dish and serve sprinkled with chopped walnuts, if liked.

RED CABBAGE AND APPLE SALAD

Illustrated in colour facing page 81

Serves 8
$\frac{1}{2}$ red cabbage (about 900 g/2 lb), finely shredded
3 eating apples
1 small garlic clove, skinned and crushed
300 ml ($\frac{1}{2}$ pint) salad oil
150 ml ($\frac{1}{4}$ pint) cider vinegar
60 ml (4 tbsp) natural yoghurt
salt and freshly ground pepper

Shred the cabbage really finely and take care not to over-blanch it, otherwise it will lose its crisp texture. Blanch the cabbage for 2–3 minutes in boiling salted water. Drain and leave to cool.

Peel, core and slice the apples and place in a bowl with the cabbage. Place the remaining ingredients in a bowl and whisk together. Pour at once over the cabbage and apple and toss together. Cover the salad and refrigerate overnight. Toss again to mix well just before serving.

LEEK AND SPROUT SALAD

Serves 4
175 g (6 oz) leeks, trimmed and thinly sliced
225 g (8 oz) Brussels sprouts, trimmed and very thinly sliced
5 ml (1 level tsp) celery seed
30 ml (2 tbsp) salad oil
30 ml (2 tbsp) distilled malt vinegar
salt and freshly ground pepper

Separate the leeks into rings and place in boiling water for 1–2 minutes. Drain and pat dry with absorbent kitchen paper. Place in a salad bowl with the Brussels sprouts. Place the celery seed, oil, vinegar and seasoning in a bowl or screw-topped jar and whisk or shake well together.

Pour the dressing over the vegetables and toss well. Cover and lightly chill in the refrigerator before serving.

CRANBERRY AND ORANGE RING

Serves 8
grated rind and juice of 1 orange
25 g (1 oz) powdered gelatine
200 ml (7 fl oz) red wine vinegar
1.25 ml ($\frac{1}{4}$ level tsp) salt
3 large oranges
two 382-g (13$\frac{1}{2}$-oz) jars cranberry sauce
celery sticks, trimmed and cut into strips, to garnish

Place the orange juice in a small bowl. Sprinkle the gelatine over it and leave to soak for 1–2 minutes. Stand the bowl in a pan of hot water and heat gently until the gelatine has dissolved. Remove from the heat. In a saucepan, gently heat the vinegar, salt and orange rind to infuse the flavours. Add the gelatine liquid, remove from the heat and leave to cool.

Peel the oranges, removing all the pith, and cut into thin slices. Cut each slice into four and combine with the cranberry sauce. Gently fold in the vinegar and gelatine liquid and pour into a 1.4-litre (2$\frac{1}{2}$-pint) plain ring mould. Chill in the refrigerator until firm.

When set, gently ease the Cranberry and orange ring away from the edges of the mould with the fingers, and dip the mould in hot water. Place a serving plate upside-down over the mould and invert the ring on to the plate. Remove the mould and fill the centre of the ring with crisp sticks of celery. This salad is ideal to serve with cold sliced meats.

BEAN SPROUT AND PRAWN SALAD

Serves 6
225 g (8 oz) bean sprouts
125 g (4 oz) mushrooms
4 sticks celery
225 g (8 oz) peeled prawns
15 ml (1 level tbsp) tomato purée
salt and freshly ground pepper
150 ml ($\frac{1}{4}$ pint) natural yoghurt
chopped fresh parsley to garnish

Wash and drain the bean sprouts. Wipe and slice the mushrooms. Wash and finely slice the celery. Mix the vegetables and prawns in a large bowl. Blend the tomato purée and plenty of seasoning into the yoghurt. Pour over the salad ingredients, fold through and leave covered for about 30 minutes. Serve garnished with plenty of chopped parsley.

COLESLAW

Serves 8
$\frac{1}{2}$ white cabbage, trimmed and finely shredded
1 large carrot, peeled and grated
1 large onion, skinned and finely chopped
45 ml (3 tbsp) chopped fresh parsley
4 sticks celery, trimmed and sliced
salt and freshly ground pepper
200 ml (7 fl oz) lemon mayonnaise (see page 103) or salad cream
watercress to garnish (optional)

In a large bowl, combine the cabbage, carrot, onion, parsley and celery, tossing well together. Season the mayonnaise or salad cream well, pour over the vegetables and toss until well coated. Cover and chill in the refrigerator for several hours before serving. Garnish with watercress, if wished. If preferred, the ingredients can be prepared beforehand and left covered. Add the dressing only 2–3 hours before serving.

CRISPY CAULIFLOWER SALAD

Serves 4
1 medium cauliflower, trimmed
1 red eating apple, cored and chopped
2 eggs, hard-boiled, shelled and chopped
50 g (2 oz) walnuts, chopped
150 ml ($\frac{1}{4}$ pint) mayonnaise (see page 102)
15 ml (1 tbsp) lemon juice
salt and freshly ground pepper

Break the cauliflower into small florets and wash and drain well. Put all the ingredients in a salad bowl, season with salt and pepper and toss well together.

POTATO SALAD

Serves 6
1 kg (2 lb) potatoes
4 spring onions, trimmed
salt and freshly ground pepper
150 ml ($\frac{1}{4}$ pint) mayonnaise (see page 102)
snipped fresh chives to garnish

Clockwise from top: Salsify and salami salad (*page 89*); Waldorf salad (*page 86*) and Fennel and orange salad (*page 96*).

Top: Red cabbage and apple salad (*page 78*); *bottom:* Dressed courgette and leek salad (*page 82*).

Place the potatoes in cold, salted water, bring to the boil and cook for 12–15 minutes until tender. Drain, remove the skins and leave until quite cold.

Cut the potatoes into small dice and place in a bowl. Finely chop the onions and add to the potatoes with salt and pepper to taste. Thin the mayonnaise, if necessary, with a little boiling water or milk, stir it into the potatoes and toss gently. Leave the salad to stand for at least 1 hour so that the flavours can blend. Sprinkle with snipped chives before serving.

CUCUMBER RAITA

Serves 4
1 cucumber
salt and freshly ground pepper
150 ml ($\frac{1}{4}$ pint) natural yoghurt
a pinch of chilli powder
a pinch of ground cumin
15 ml (1 tbsp) chopped coriander leaves *(optional)*

Coarsely grate the cucumber on to a plate, sprinkle with salt and leave to stand for 30 minutes. Drain well. Put the yoghurt in a small bowl and stir in the chilli powder, ground cumin and cucumber. Season well with salt and pepper and chill in the refrigerator before serving garnished with coriander, if liked.

MOULDED CUCUMBER AND CARROT RING

Serves 4
600-ml (1-pint) packet lemon jelly
150 ml ($\frac{1}{4}$ pint) boiling water
150 ml ($\frac{1}{4}$ pint) cider vinegar
150 ml ($\frac{1}{4}$ pint) white wine
100 g (4 oz) carrots, coarsely grated
175 g (6 oz) cucumber, diced

Break up the jelly tablet, place it in a bowl and pour over the boiling water. Stir until the jelly has dissolved. Add the vinegar and white wine. Chill the jelly in the refrigerator until it is the consistency of unbeaten egg white.

Mix the carrot and cucumber together and fold it into the setting jelly. Pour into a 750-ml ($1\frac{1}{4}$-pint) plain ring mould and chill until firm.

To serve, quickly dip the mould into hot water. Place a serving plate upside-down over the mould and invert the ring on to the plate. Serve this salad with cold sliced meats.

DRESSED COURGETTE AND LEEK SALAD

Illustrated in colour facing page 81

Serves 4
350 g (12 oz) courgettes, trimmed and sliced
275 g (10 oz) leeks, trimmed and sliced
45 ml (3 tbsp) fresh herb vinaigrette (see page 100)

Blanch the courgettes in boiling water for 1 minute. Drain, pat dry with absorbent kitchen paper and place in a bowl. Blanch the leeks in boiling water for about 2 minutes. Drain well and add to the courgettes. Pour the dressing over the vegetables while they are still warm. Toss lightly, then chill in the refrigerator before serving.

MANGE TOUT SALAD

Serves 4
225 g (8 oz) mange tout, trimmed
30 ml (2 tbsp) vegetable oil
1 cucumber
30 ml (2 tbsp) single cream or top of the milk
45 ml (3 tbsp) French dressing (see page 100)
1 round lettuce
chopped fresh parsley and mint to garnish

Cook the mange tout in boiling salted water for about 4 minutes, drain and return to the pan. While still hot, add the vegetable oil and stir until well coated. Leave to cool.

Cut the cucumber into 5-cm (2-inch) sticks. Beat the cream or top of the milk into the French dressing. Place the lettuce, shredded if liked, the mange tout and the cucumber in a salad bowl, pour over the dressing and toss until evenly coated. Sprinkle with parsley and mint and serve immediately.

SALADE AUX NOIX

Serves 6
1 firm-hearted lettuce, washed
50 g (2 oz) walnuts, roughly chopped
120 ml (8 tbsp) French dressing (see page 100)

Shred the lettuce finely and place it in a bowl with the walnuts. Pour the dressing over and toss well just before serving.

CELERIAC AND CARROT SALAD

The slight celery flavour of celeriac adds interest to many salads. Celeriac discolors quickly, so grate it straight into the dressing.

Serves 6
135 ml (9 tbsp) French dressing (see page 100)
700 g (1½ lb) celeriac
450 g (1 lb) old carrots, peeled and grated
salt and freshly ground pepper
chopped fresh parsley to garnish

Place the dressing in a bowl. Thickly peel the celeriac with a sharp knife or potato peeler and coarsely grate it straight into the dressing. Add the carrots and mix well. Cover the bowl tightly with cling film and refrigerate for several hours. To serve, stir, season and spoon on to individual plates. Sprinkle with parsley and serve at once.

CELERIAC RÉMOULADE

Serves 6
1 large head celeriac
30 ml (2 tbsp) lemon juice
300 ml (½ pint) mayonnaise (see page 102)
salt and freshly ground pepper
30 ml (2 tbsp) snipped fresh chives
30 ml (2 level tbsp) French mustard
1 lettuce
chopped fresh parsley to garnish

Peel and coarsely grate the celeriac and toss in the lemon juice to prevent discoloration. Add the remaining ingredients, except the lettuce and parsley, and mix well together. Serve on a bed of lettuce, sprinkled with chopped parsley.

PASTA SIDE SALAD

Serves 8
225 g (8 oz) large shell pasta
1 medium cauliflower (about 700 g/1½ lb trimmed weight)
225 g (8 oz) green pepper
30 ml (2 tbsp) vegetable oil
2 medium onions, skinned and finely sliced
2 lemons
5 ml (1 level tsp) dried thyme
312-g (11-oz) can corn niblets, drained
100 ml (4 fl oz) double cream
salt and freshly ground pepper

Cook the pasta in boiling salted water for 10–12 minutes until tender. Drain well, rinse in cold running water and drain again. Break the cauliflower into small florets and cook for 5 minutes in boiling salted water. Drain, refresh in cold water and drain again. Halve, seed and finely slice the pepper. Blanch in boiling salted water for 2 minutes and drain.

Heat the oil in a frying pan, add the onion and pepper and fry for 2–3 minutes until beginning to soften. Remove from the heat. Finely grate the rind of the lemons into the pan, then stir in the thyme, corn and cream. Leave to cool. In a large bowl fold together all the ingredients, season well and serve on individual serving plates or in natural scallop shells.

WATERCRESS AND APPLE SALAD

Serves 6
2 bunches watercress
90 ml (6 tbsp) French dressing (see page 100)
3 eating apples
25 g (1 oz) shelled walnuts, finely chopped

Dress the salad at the last minute to keep it crisp. Trim any roots from the watercress, wash and drain it well, and pat it dry on absorbent kitchen paper. Pour the dressing into a bowl. Quarter and core the apples and slice them into the dressing. Stir immediately to prevent the apples discoloring. Add the walnuts with the watercress sprigs and toss lightly in the dressing. Spoon into a serving bowl and serve immediately.

CAULIFLOWER, DATE AND BANANA SALAD

Serves 4
350 g (12 oz) cauliflower florets
2 bananas
juice of $\frac{1}{2}$ lemon
150 ml ($\frac{1}{4}$ pint) lemon mayonnaise (see page 103)
50 g (2 oz) whole dates, stoned
75 g (3 oz) endive leaves

Blanch the cauliflower florets in boiling salted water for 3 minutes. Drain and plunge at once into cold water. Drain again and pat dry with absorbent kitchen paper.

Peel the bananas and cut into 0.5-cm ($\frac{1}{4}$-inch) slices. Toss in the lemon juice. Add two thirds of the banana to the cauliflower. Mash the remaining banana and add to the mayonnaise. Lightly combine the cauliflower and mayonnaise mixtures. Scissor-snip the dates and add to the mixture.

Cover the base of four small side plates with endive. Divide the cauliflower mayonnaise equally and spoon into the centre of the endive. Chill for 30 minutes before serving. This is delicious with cold roast chicken and ham.

TOSSED ITALIAN SALAD

Serves 6
2 medium red peppers, seeded and thinly sliced
2 medium green peppers, seeded and thinly sliced
450 g (1 lb) courgettes, trimmed and sliced
1 small onion, skinned and finely chopped
4 large firm tomatoes, skinned and quartered
50 g (2 oz) stuffed olives
freshly ground black pepper
a few snipped fresh chives
135 ml (9 tbsp) garlic vinaigrette (see page 101)

Blanch the peppers, courgettes and onion separately in fast-boiling salted water. Boil the peppers for 3 minutes, the courgettes for about 4 minutes, until the centres look transparent, and the onion for 1 minute. Drain, cool quickly in cold water and drain again. Pat dry with absorbent kitchen paper.

Combine the blanched ingredients with the tomatoes and olives in a serving bowl. Sprinkle well with pepper.

Add the chives to the garlic vinaigrette and pour over the salad. Toss lightly and chill in the refrigerator before serving.

POTATO AND BEAN VINAIGRETTE

Serves 6
900 g (2 lb) small new potatoes
450 g (1 lb) French beans
200 ml (7 fl oz) French dressing (see page 100)
2 eggs, hard-boiled

Scrape the potatoes. Top and tail the French beans, halve, wash and drain. Cook the vegetables together in boiling salted water for 10–15 minutes until tender. Drain, transfer to a bowl and immediately stir in the French dressing. Cool, then cover and refrigerate.

Remove from the refrigerator about 30 minutes before serving. Shell and chop the eggs, then stir into the salad and serve.

BANGKOK SALAD

Bean sprouts are now a popular vegetable which can be quickly grown at home.

Serves 2–3
175 g (6 oz) bean sprouts, washed and drained
1 red pepper, seeded and sliced
15 ml (1 tbsp) lemon juice
15 ml (1 tbsp) distilled malt vinegar

Mix the bean sprouts and pepper together in a serving dish. Place the lemon juice and vinegar in a bowl or screw-topped jar and whisk or shake well together. Pour over the sprouts and pepper and toss together. Leave to stand for about 30 minutes before serving.

WALDORF SALAD

Illustrated in colour facing page 80

Serves 4
450 g (1 lb) eating apples
lemon juice
5 ml (1 level tsp) sugar
150 ml ($\frac{1}{4}$ pint) mayonnaise (see page 102)
$\frac{1}{2}$ head celery, trimmed and sliced
50 g (2 oz) walnuts, chopped
1 lettuce
a few walnut halves to garnish (optional)

Peel and core the apples, slice one and dice the rest. Dip the slices in lemon juice to prevent discoloration. Toss the diced apples in 30 ml (2 tbsp) lemon juice, the sugar and 15 ml (1 tbsp) mayonnaise and leave to stand for about 30 minutes.

Just before serving, add the celery, walnuts and remaining mayonnaise and toss together. Serve in a bowl lined with lettuce leaves and garnish with the apple slices and a few whole walnuts, if liked.

BEAN SPROUT AND BROWN RICE SALAD

The nutty taste of brown rice mixed with crisp, juicy bean sprouts makes an interesting salad accompaniment.

Serves 6
225 g (8 oz) long grain brown rice
225 g (8 oz) fresh bean sprouts
1 large green pepper
90 ml (6 tbsp) French dressing (see page 100)

Cook the rice in a large pan of boiling salted water for about 30 minutes until just tender. Drain and rinse through with hot water. Wash the bean sprouts and drain well. Halve the pepper, discard the seeds, dice and mix in a bowl with the bean sprouts and rice. Spoon the dressing over the salad and stir well. Cover and chill for 2 hours before serving.

JELLIED BEETROOT AND APPLE SALAD

Serves 4–6
600-ml (1-pint) packet red jelly
300 ml ($\frac{1}{2}$ pint) boiling water
150 ml ($\frac{1}{4}$ pint) distilled malt vinegar
30 ml (2 tbsp) lemon juice
450 g (1 lb) cooked beetroot, skinned
2 eating apples
50 g (2 oz) walnut halves

Break up the jelly tablet, place in a bowl, pour over the boiling water and stir until dissolved. Mix together the vinegar and lemon juice, make up to 300 ml ($\frac{1}{2}$ pint) with cold water and add to the hot jelly liquid.

Slice or dice the cooked beetroot. Peel, core and slice the apples. Place the walnut halves in the base of a 1.1-litre (2-pint) ring mould and add the beetroot and apple in layers. Pour on the liquid jelly and leave in the refrigerator for about 3 hours until set. To serve, unmould on to a flat plate.

CAESAR SALAD

This famous American salad is fun to make and deliciously crispy with the addition of garlic croûtons.

Serves 4
1 large garlic clove, skinned and crushed
150 ml ($\frac{1}{4}$ pint) olive oil
75 g (3 oz) stale white bread
1 Cos lettuce
salt and freshly ground pepper
1 egg
30 ml (2 tbsp) lemon juice
25 g (1 oz) Parmesan cheese, grated
8 anchovies, finely chopped

Add the garlic to the oil and leave to stand for 30 minutes. Cut the bread into 0.5-cm ($\frac{1}{4}$-inch) dice. Heat a little of the garlic oil in a frying pan and fry the bread until golden brown on all sides. Lift from the pan and drain.

Wash and dry the lettuce leaves and tear into bite-sized pieces. Place in a salad bowl. Pour over the remaining garlic oil and toss until the leaves are completely coated. Season well. Boil the egg for 1 minute only, break it into the salad and toss well. Add the lemon juice, cheese, anchovies and croûtons and give a final toss. Serve immediately.

ENDIVE, ORANGE AND WALNUT SALAD

Serves 8
2 endive
6 oranges
25 g (1 oz) walnut halves
15 ml (1 level tbsp) caster sugar
150 ml ($\frac{1}{4}$ pint) corn oil
60 ml (4 tbsp) lemon juice
salt and freshly ground pepper

Trim the base of the endive, discard any outside wilted or damaged leaves and wash and dry thoroughly. Tear into pieces and place in a salad bowl. Grate the rind of one orange into a bowl and squeeze in the juice.

Using a serrated knife, remove the peel and all the white pith from the remaining oranges. Segment the oranges, discarding as much of the membrane as possible, and the pips. Add the segments to the endive. Add the walnuts, cover and keep refrigerated.

Just before serving, combine the sugar with the reserved orange juice and rind. Gradually beat in the oil and stir in the lemon juice. Season well. Spoon the dressing over the endive and toss the mixture lightly.

ICEBERG LETTUCE WITH AVOCADO AND BACON

Serves 6
4 rashers lean bacon, rinded
1 iceberg lettuce
$\frac{1}{2}$ medium cucumber
1 avocado
juice of $\frac{1}{2}$ a lemon
150 ml ($\frac{1}{4}$ pint) French dressing (see page 100)

Fry or grill the bacon rashers until very crisp, then drain, cool and crumble into small pieces. Wash the lettuce, shred finely and place in a salad bowl. Thinly slice the cucumber and add to the salad bowl.

Halve, stone and peel the avocado, then slice and toss in the lemon juice. Add the avocado to the salad, pour over the French dressing and toss well together. Sprinkle over the bacon pieces and serve immediately.

SALSIFY AND SALAMI SALAD

Illustrated in colour facing page 80
An interesting salad to brighten up the dull winter days.

Serves 4
450 g (1 lb) salsify, trimmed and peeled
300 ml ($\frac{1}{2}$ pint) chicken stock
50 g (2 oz) salami, in one piece
4 large tomatoes, skinned
50 g (2 oz) black olives, stoned
120 ml (8 tbsp) French dressing (see page 100)

Place the salsify in a saucepan with the stock, Cover, bring to the boil and cook for 15–20 minutes until tender. Drain well and leave until cold. Cut into thick slices and place in a salad bowl.

Cut the salami into small pieces and the tomatoes into wedges. Add to the salad bowl with the black olives. Pour the French dressing over the salad, toss well and leave for 30 minutes before serving.

GREEN SALAD

Use two or more green salad ingredients, such as lettuce, mustard and cress, watercress, endive, chicory, peppers, cucumber, cabbage, etc. Wash and drain them well and, just before serving, toss lightly in a bowl with French dressing (see page 100), adding a little finely chopped onion if liked.

Sprinkle with chopped fresh parsley, chives, mint, tarragon or other herbs, as available.

SPINACH SALAD

Serves 4
225 g (8 oz) fresh young spinach leaves
8 rashers streaky bacon, rinded and chopped
45 ml (3 tbsp) vegetable oil
2 large slices white bread, cut into 1-cm ($\frac{1}{2}$-inch) cubes
1 garlic clove, skinned and crushed
15 ml (1 tbsp) lemon juice
salt and freshly ground pepper

Wash the spinach thoroughly. Dry well and shred the spinach into small strips, discarding any tough stems. Place in a salad bowl.

Fry the bacon in its own fat for about 5 minutes until crisp and golden brown. Remove from the pan and drain on absorbent kitchen paper. Add 15 ml (1 tbsp) oil to the pan and fry the bread until golden brown. Stir the garlic into the pan with the bread croûtons, then drain the croûtons on absorbent kitchen paper.

Place the remaining oil, the lemon juice and seasoning in a bowl or screw-topped jar and whisk or shake well together. Pour the dressing over the spinach, toss well and scatter the croûtons and bacon on top.

LETTUCE WEDGES

Serves 6
6 spring onions, trimmed
$\frac{1}{2}$ small red pepper, seeded and finely chopped
$\frac{1}{2}$ small green pepper, seeded and finely chopped
120 ml (8 tbsp) French dressing (see page 100)
1 large crisp 'hearty' lettuce, eg Webb's Wonder or Cos

Snip the onions into thin rounds. Add the onion and pepper to the French dressing and leave to marinate for several hours.

Divide the lettuce into six wedge shapes, discarding any damaged outside leaves, and wash well. Drain, pat dry and arrange spirally in a shallow salad bowl. Spoon over the dressing just before serving.

MIXED BEAN SALAD

Serves 6

275 g (10 oz) mixed dried beans, eg aduki, red kidney, black or haricots, soaked overnight

2.5 ml ($\frac{1}{2}$ level tsp) ground coriander

100 ml (4 fl oz) French dressing (see page 100)

1 small onion, skinned and very finely sliced

salt and freshly ground pepper

Drain the beans, place in a saucepan and cover with fresh water. Bring to the boil, boil for 10 minutes, then cover and simmer for about 1 hour, until tender. Alternatively, cook in a pressure cooker at HIGH (15 lb) pressure for 15–20 minutes. (If aduki beans are included, add them halfway through the cooking time.) Drain and place in a large bowl.

Add the coriander to the French dressing and pour over the beans while they are still warm. Toss thoroughly and leave to cool.

Add the onion to the beans, stir well and adjust the seasoning. Chill in the refrigerator and transfer to a salad bowl or individual serving plates.

TZAZIKI

Traditionally, this Greek salad is made with Greek yoghurt which is much thicker in consistency than ours—if you are unable to buy this, choose a firm set natural yoghurt if possible. If you like garlic, a small crushed clove greatly enhances this dish.

Serves 4

$\frac{1}{2}$ medium cucumber

150 ml ($\frac{1}{4}$ pint) natural yoghurt

15 ml (1 tbsp) chopped fresh mint

salt and freshly ground pepper

Finely dice the cucumber, place in a colander, sprinkle with salt and leave to stand for 30 minutes to draw out the juices. Rinse, drain well and dry with absorbent kitchen paper. Place in a serving bowl. Pour over the yoghurt, add the mint, season and mix well. Cover and chill before serving.

LEMON-DRESSED AVOCADO SALAD

Serves 6
½ small cucumber
2 ripe avocados
150 ml (¼ pint) vegetable oil
60 ml (4 tbsp) lemon juice
10 ml (2 tsp) thin honey
salt and freshly ground pepper
4 sticks celery, trimmed and thinly sliced
50 g (2 oz) salted peanuts
paprika to garnish

Skin and dice the cucumber, place in a colander, sprinkle with salt and leave for 20 minutes to draw out the juices. Rinse and drain well, then dry on absorbent kitchen paper. Stone, peel and slice the avocados thickly.

Place the oil, lemon juice, honey and seasoning in a bowl or screw-topped jar and whisk or shake well together. Place the celery and peanuts in a bowl with the cucumber and avocado, pour over the dressing and toss well. Pile into a serving dish, dust with paprika pepper and serve immediately.

DILL CUCUMBER

This Scandinavian way of serving cucumber is very refreshing and is particularly good with fish.

Serves 4
2 cucumbers
10 ml (2 level tsp) salt
100 ml (4 fl oz) white wine vinegar
freshly ground pepper
a few sprigs of fresh dill, chopped

Peel the cucumbers and slice in half lengthways. Scoop out the seeds with a teaspoon and slice the cucumbers very thinly. Place in a bowl with the salt and vinegar and leave to stand for 30 minutes, turning occasionally.

Drain the cucumber well and place it in a clean tea towel. Squeeze to remove all excess moisture. Place in a serving bowl and add the pepper and dill. Cover and chill in the refrigerator before use. Serve with rollmop herrings or use on Danish open sandwiches.

MUSHROOM, CUCUMBER AND CORIANDER SALAD

This simple salad owes its distinctive flavour to coriander. When in season, use finely chopped leaves of the fresh herb.

Serves 8
450 g (1 lb) button mushrooms, wiped and sliced
120 ml (8 tbsp) sunflower oil
75 ml (5 tbsp) white wine vinegar
10 ml (2 level tsp) ground coriander
salt and freshly ground pepper
1 large cucumber

Place the mushrooms in a large serving bowl. Place the oil, vinegar, coriander and salt and pepper to taste in a bowl or screw-topped jar and whisk or shake well together. Pour over the mushrooms and leave to marinate for about 30 minutes. Thinly slice the cucumber, cover and set aside.

Just before serving, drain off any liquid from the cucumber and fold carefully into the mushrooms. Add more salt and pepper if necessary.

AUSTRALIAN GARDEN SALAD

This is a very colourful salad that can be served the year round. The cauliflower can be blanched, but don't overcook it.

Serves 6
½ small cauliflower, trimmed
1 large onion, skinned
1 cucumber
1 large green pepper
1 large red pepper
225 g (8 oz) young spinach
10 ml (2 level tsp) sugar
5 ml (1 level tsp) paprika
5 ml (1 level tsp) dried thyme
5 ml (1 tsp) chopped fresh parsley
salt and freshly ground pepper
150 ml (¼ pint) French dressing (see page 100)

Soak the cauliflower in salted water for 30 minutes. Rinse and drain, then divide into small florets. Dice the onion and cucumber. Seed the peppers and cut into thin strips. Wash and dry the spinach and chop roughly. In a large bowl, combine the prepared ingredients with the sugar, herbs and seasonings. Pour over the dressing and toss well.

RED BEAN AND CAULIFLOWER SALAD

Serves 8

250 g (9 oz) dried red kidney beans, soaked overnight
2 medium cauliflowers, trimmed
175 g (6 oz) leeks, trimmed
120 ml (8 tbsp) French dressing (see page 100)

Drain the kidney beans, place in a saucepan, cover with fresh water, bring to the boil and boil for 10 minutes, then simmer, covered, for 1½–2 hours until tender. Drain well and place in a bowl.

Break the cauliflower into small florets. Blanch in boiling salted water for 3 minutes, drain and cool under cold running water. Halve the leeks lengthways and finely slice. Wash well and add to the beans with the cauliflower. Pour the dressing over, toss well together, cover and chill in the refrigerator for several hours. Turn into a salad bowl to serve.

WHOLE POTATO SALAD

The dressing really flavours the potatoes if it is poured over while they are still warm.

Serves 4–6

700 g (1½ lb) new potatoes, scrubbed
120 ml (8 tbsp) French dressing (see page 100)
chopped fresh parsley or snipped chives

Cook the potatoes in boiling salted water for 10–15 minutes until tender. Drain and, while still warm, remove the skins from the potatoes. Place the potatoes in a serving dish and immediately pour on the dressing. Leave to cool for 1–2 hours. Serve sprinkled with parsley or chives.

RICE SALAD

Serves 8

450 g (1 lb) long grain rice
two 227-g (8-oz) packets frozen mixed vegetables (peas, sweetcorn and peppers)
150 ml (¼ pint) French dressing (see page 100)
16 stuffed olives, sliced (optional)

Boil the rice in plenty of salted water for 10 minutes until tender, then drain and rinse in cold water. Drain well and place in a large serving bowl.

Cook the frozen vegetables as directed on the packet, drain and rinse in cold water, then drain again and add to the rice. Stir well together. Add the French dressing and toss the rice mixture well together. Add the sliced olives, if liked.

WHOLEWHEAT AND APRICOT SALAD

Serves 6–8
225 g (8 oz) wholewheat grain
125 g (4 oz) dried apricots, washed
3 sticks celery, trimmed and sliced
90 ml (6 tbsp) French dressing (see page 100)

Soak the wholewheat overnight in plenty of cold water. Drain and place in a large saucepan of boiling water. Simmer gently for 25 minutes, or until the grains are tender but retain a little bite. Drain well, rinse under cold running water and place in a bowl.

Snip the apricots into small pieces and add to the wholewheat with the celery. Pour the dressing over the salad and toss well. Cover and chill in the refrigerator for several hours. Stir again just before serving.

ORANGE RICE SALAD

Serves 8
350 g (12 oz) long grain rice
900 ml (1½ pints) water
5 ml (1 level tsp) salt
grated rind of 1 orange
75 g (3 oz) seedless raisins
75 ml (5 tbsp) French dressing (see page 100)

Put the rice, water and salt in a large saucepan, bring to the boil and stir once. Lower the heat, cover tightly and simmer for 10 minutes. Add the orange rind and raisins and cook, covered, for about 5 minutes more. Test the rice—if it is not quite tender, or if the liquid is not completely absorbed, replace the lid and cook for a few minutes more. Drain well and turn into a serving dish. While the mixture is still hot, add the French dressing and stir well. Chill in the refrigerator before serving.

FENNEL AND WATERCRESS SALAD

Serves 6
700 g (1½ lb) Florence fennel
lemon juice
1 large bunch watercress
90 ml (6 tbsp) olive oil
45 ml (3 tbsp) white wine vinegar
salt and freshly ground pepper

Trim the root end off the fennel bulbs and cut away the tops of the stalks and any feathery leaves. Reserve the best leaves for garnish. Slice the fennel thinly, discarding any discolored pieces. Blanch the fennel in boiling salted water, with a good squeeze of lemon juice added, for 2 minutes only. Drain well.

Meanwhile, wash, drain and dry the watercress. Separate the sprigs from the stalks. Finely chop the stalks and refrigerate the sprigs in a polythene bag until required.

In a bowl, mix the oil, vinegar, chopped watercress and seasoning. Add the drained fennel and stir to coat. Cover with cling film and refrigerate for several hours. Just before serving, stir in the watercress sprigs and garnish with snipped fennel leaves.

INSALATA DI FINOCCHI E ARANCI (FENNEL AND ORANGE SALAD)

Illustrated in colour facing page 80

This salad makes a very refreshing accompaniment to roast pork or game. For best results, use olive oil for the French dressing.

Serves 4–6
2 bulbs fennel (about 450 g/1 lb)
4 medium oranges
150 ml (¼ pint) French dressing (see page 100)

Remove any feathery leaves from the fennel bulbs, reserving a few for garnish. Thinly slice the fennel vertically, removing any brown, withered pieces. Wash the slices well, drain and arrange on a flat serving dish.

Using a serrated knife, cut away all the peel and white pith from the oranges and cut into segments, discarding as much of the membrane as possible, and the pips. While doing this, hold the oranges over a bowl to catch any juice. Arrange the orange segments over the fennel. Combine the orange juice with the French dressing and spoon over the salad. Garnish with reserved fennel leaves.

DRESSING THE SALAD

Every salad should be dressed, either with a mayonnaise, vinaigrette, a simple dressing of lemon juice or any of the exciting variety to be found in this chapter.

The dressing can make or mar a salad. The most usual mistake is to use too much dressing, swamping the salad instead of making it appetising. No surplus dressing should be seen at the bottom of the bowl—there should be just sufficient clinging to the salad ingredients to flavour them. Before dressing a salad, make sure all the ingredients are dry so that the dressing will cling to the salad and will not be diluted and make a watery salad.

In general it is better to dress a salad just before serving, while some benefit from the ingredients being allowed to marinate in the dressing and some salads of cooked vegetables will absorb the flavour of the dressing better if it is added while the vegetables are still warm and left to chill. If you wish to toss the salad at the table, mix the dressing in the bottom of the salad bowl, cross the servers over it and pile the salad loosely on top. It is then simple to toss the salad and dressing together at the table.

It is best to dress a salad in a large bowl and then spoon it into the individual bowls after tossing well. Always serve and toss salad in a chilled bowl to preserve its freshness.

OILS

OLIVE OIL Although pricey, olive oil is probably the most popular for salad dressings. It is graded according to the method of extraction. The finest is virgin oil, pressed first at room temperature. After that, temperature and pressure are increased to force out more oil. Taste and colour vary according to pressing—very pale for virgin, yellow for first pressing, through to yellowy green or green for second. A blend of olive oils usually works out cheaper.

GROUNDNUT OIL This is made from peanuts. It is light and bland but can be used for salad dressings.

SALAD OIL This is a name that doesn't mean much as most oils can be used for salad providing the flavour is acceptable. It is usually groundnut oil or, sometimes, a blend of olive oil. Check the label to see what you are getting. If it says *arachide*, don't think it's something fancy—it's French for groundnut.

SOYA BEAN OIL This is made from beans grown mainly in the USA. Soya beans are the world's leading source of vegetable oil. Although it has a strong flavour, it is often used for salad dressing.

BLENDED VEGETABLE OIL This is derived from the seeds of different plants grown in different countries. Rapeseed is one of the main types used. It is relatively cheap because manufacturers buy up seeds at advantageous prices. This means that the blend is continually changing, although the flavour remains constant, and the exact composition cannot be stated on the container.

CORN OR MAIZE OIL This can be used for salad dressings although it has a bland flavour.

SUNFLOWER OIL This is becoming more popular. It has a pleasant taste and blends well in salad dressing. It has a particularly high ratio of polyunsaturated fats.

SAFFLOWER SEED OIL This is also bland and light with a high poly-unsaturated fat content. It is mainly sold through specialist health food shops.

SESAME SEED OIL Expensive but delicious. It is used mainly for making salad dressings although its distinctive nutty flavour limits its use.

WALNUT OIL Too expensive for general cooking but excellent for salad dressings. Its delicious nutty flavour makes it an unusual salad dressing. A favourite with the French not often found here but occasionally sold in specialist food shops.

GARLIC OIL

2 garlic cloves, skinned and crushed
300 ml ($\frac{1}{2}$ pint) vegetable oil

Use for making mayonnaise and salad dressings. Place the garlic and oil together in a screw-topped bottle or airtight container. Shake the container and then leave in a warm place for 2–3 weeks, shaking the container occasionally. This allows time for the flavours to infuse. Strain before using.

VINEGARS

Although red and white wine vinegars and cider vinegar are probably the first choice, the sharper flavoured malt vinegars are all suitable for making salad dressings. The type of vinegar has been indicated in the recipes to compliment the ingredients in the salads but can be varied. Each has its own distinctive flavour and which you use is a matter of personal choice. Herb and fruit vinegars can also be used (see the recipes below).

HERB VINEGARS

Fill bottles with sprigs of leaves from freshly gathered herbs such as rosemary, tarragon, mint, thyme, marjoram, basil, dill, sage or parsley. Use either a mixture of herbs or just one variety. Fill the bottles with a good quality red or white wine vinegar, then cover and leave in a cool, dry place for about 6 weeks. Strain through muslin. Taste and add more vinegar if the flavour is too strong. Pour into bottles and seal with airtight and vinegar-proof tops.

FRUIT VINEGARS

These are usually made with raspberries, blackberries or blackcurrants.
Place the washed fruit in a bowl and break it up slightly with the back of a wooden spoon. For each 450 g (1 lb) fruit, pour in 600 ml (1 pint) distilled malt or white wine vinegar. Cover with a clean cloth and leave to stand for 3–4 days, stirring occasionally. Strain through muslin and add 450 g (1 lb) sugar to each 600 ml (1 pint). Boil for 10 minutes, then cool, strain again, pour into bottles and seal with airtight and vinegar-proof tops. Add a few whole pieces of fruit to each bottle, if liked. Herb and fruit vinegars will keep for years if stored in a cool, dark place.

GARLIC VINEGAR

3 garlic cloves, skinned and sliced
600 ml (1 pint) distilled malt vinegar

P lace the garlic in a warm bottle. Heat the vinegar in a saucepan and bring to the boil. Pour on to the garlic and leave to cool. Seal with a vinegar-proof top and leave in a cool place for about 6 weeks. Taste, and if sufficiently flavoured, strain through a nylon sieve. Re-bottle and seal with an airtight, vinegar-proof top.

SAUCE VINAIGRETTE
(FRENCH DRESSING)

90 ml (6 tbsp) oil (see page 98)
45 ml (3 tbsp) vinegar (see below) or lemon juice
2.5 ml ($\frac{1}{2}$ level tsp) sugar
2.5 ml ($\frac{1}{2}$ level tsp) mustard, eg wholegrain, Dijon, French, or mustard powder
salt and freshly ground pepper

P lace all the ingredients in a bowl or screw-topped jar and whisk or shake together until well blended. The oil separates out on standing, so whisk or shake the dressing again if necessary immediately before use.

The dressing can be stored in a bottle or screw-topped jar for up to a year in the refrigerator, but shake it up vigorously just before serving.

Note The proportion of oil to vinegar can be varied according to taste. Here it is in the ratio of two to one. Use less oil if a sharper dressing is preferred.

Wine, herb, cider or flavoured vinegars (see page 99), or lemon juice, may be used, or use a mixture of half vinegar and half lemon juice.

This recipe makes 135 ml (9 tbsp) dressing. If a recipe calls for 150 ml ($\frac{1}{4}$ pint) dressing, add an extra 15 ml (1 tbsp) oil.

VARIATIONS
The following variations are made by adding the ingredients to the above basic French dressing. Shake or whisk well to combine.

Fresh herb vinaigrette Add 15 ml (1 tbsp) chopped fresh parsley or 15 ml (1 tbsp) chopped fresh mint or 10 ml (2 tsp) snipped fresh chives, or a mixture of all three.

Mustard vinaigrette Add 15 ml (1 tbsp) wholegrain mustard.

Bombay dressing Add a large pinch of curry powder, 1 finely chopped hard-boiled egg and 10 ml (2 tsp) chopped onion.

Curry vinaigrette Add 5 ml (1 level tsp) curry powder.

Anchovy vinaigrette Add 15 ml (1 tbsp) finely chopped anchovies.

Blue cheese vinaigrette Add 25 g (1 oz) blue cheese, crumbled.

Garlic vinaigrette Add 2 garlic cloves, skinned and crushed.

Piquant vinaigrette Add 10 ml (2 tsp) chopped fresh parsley, 10 ml (2 tsp) chopped gherkins or capers and 10 ml (2 tsp) chopped stuffed olives.

Olive vinaigrette Add 30 ml (2 tbsp) finely sliced or chopped stuffed olives.

Tomato juice vinaigrette Add 120 ml (8 tbsp) tomato juice and 30 ml (2 tbsp) chopped fresh parsley or mint.

MAYONNAISE

What 'mayonnaise' really means is not clear; some people maintain it's a corruption of the French word *magnonaise* from *manier* meaning to stir, some that it comes from *moyeunaise*, derived from the old French word *moyeu* meaning middle or yolk of the egg, and others that it is named after Napoleon's Irish general, McMahon. But the end product is not in dispute: it is an emulsion of oil and raw eggs (either whole or, more usually, yolks only) with seasoning, vinegar or lemon juice, used to turn plain food into a gourmet's delight.

Choice of ingredients The flavour of mayonnaise varies according to its ingredients and is a matter of personal taste. Wine vinegar is less sharp than malt vinegar; lemon juice gives a distinctive fresh tang. Any bland oil, such as corn or groundnut oil, can be used successfully; olive oil, apart from its high cost, has a flavour that some people find too marked and, incidentally, produces a slightly thicker mayonnaise. Either whole eggs or egg yolks can be used—one whole egg produces the same quantity as two yolks, but bear in mind that whole eggs give a lighter texture and colour and the mayonnaise is more likely to separate than if it were made with yolks only.

Rules for success All the ingredients must be at warm room temperature—take an egg from the refrigerator or oil from a cold larder and you can guarantee the mayonnaise will curdle. If necessary, warm the bowl and utensils that you'll be using. Mix the egg with the dry ingredients (see basic ingredients on page 102) and 5 ml (1 tsp) vinegar or lemon juice; add the first 30 ml (2 tbsp) oil drop by drop. The oil and the moisture in the egg will not mix naturally but when beaten vigorously the oil breaks down into small droplets which are coated by the protein molecules in the yolk to form an emulsion. Adding too much oil too quickly forms a separate layer and the mixture curdles. Once you have beaten in the first 30 ml (2 tbsp) oil, the rest can be added in a thin stream or 15 ml (1 tbsp) at a time. Keep beating vigorously. If at any time the mayonnaise becomes too thick, it can be thinned down with 5 ml (1 tsp) of the vinegar or lemon juice (the rest should be beaten in at the end).

Rescue remedies If the mayonnaise separates while you are making it, there are ways to save it, all involving beating the curdled mixture into a fresh base.

This base can be any one of the following: 5 ml (1 tsp) hot water; 5 ml (1 tsp) vinegar or lemon juice; 5 ml (1 tsp) Dijon mustard or 2.5 ml ($\frac{1}{2}$ level tsp) mustard powder (the mayonnaise will taste more strongly of mustard than usual); or an egg yolk. Add the curdled mixture to the base, beating hard. When the mixture is smooth, continue adding the oil as above. (If you use an extra egg yolk you may find that you need to add a little extra oil.)

The right utensils Mayonnaise can be made with anything from a fork, balloon whisk, rotary whisk or electric hand mixer to a blender or food processor.

Making mayonnaise in a blender or food processor Most blenders and food processors need at least a two-egg quantity in order to ensure that the blades are covered, and a food processor really comes into its own when you are making large quantities. Put the yolks or whole eggs, seasoning and half the vinegar or lemon juice into the blender goblet or food processor bowl and blend together. If your machine has a variable speed control, run it at a slow speed. Add the oil gradually through the top of the blender goblet or the funnel of the processor while the machine is running. Add the remaining vinegar and check the seasoning.

Storing mayonnaise Homemade mayonnaise does not keep as long as bought varieties because it lacks their added emulsifiers, stabilisers and preservatives. The freshness of the eggs and oil used and the temperature at which it is stored also affect its keeping qualities. However, mayonnaise should keep for 3–4 days at room temperature and for at least a month in a screw-topped glass jar in the refrigerator.

Serving mayonnaise Allow mayonnaise to come to room temperature before serving.

Bought mayonnaise It is always worth making your own mayonnaise but if you do not have the time, bought mayonnaise can be used. Use in the same way as homemade mayonnaise.

CLASSIC MAYONNAISE

1 egg yolk
2.5 ml ($\frac{1}{2}$ level tsp) mustard powder or 5 ml (1 level tsp) Dijon mustard
2.5 ml ($\frac{1}{2}$ level tsp) salt
1.25 ml ($\frac{1}{4}$ level tsp) freshly ground pepper
2.5 ml ($\frac{1}{2}$ level tsp) sugar
15 ml (1 tbsp) white wine vinegar or lemon juice
about 150 ml ($\frac{1}{4}$ pint) oil (see page 98)

Put the egg yolk into a bowl with the mustard, seasoning, sugar and 5 ml (1 tsp) of the vinegar or lemon juice. Mix thoroughly, then add the oil drop by drop, stirring briskly with a wooden spoon the whole time, or whisking constantly, until the sauce is thick and smooth. If it becomes too thick, add a little more of the vinegar or lemon juice. When all the oil has been added, add the vinegar or lemon juice gradually and mix thoroughly.

If a recipe requires thin mayonnaise, thin it down with a little warm water, single cream, vinegar or lemon juice just before serving. Add the extra liquid slowly—too much will spoil the consistency.

Note To keep the bowl firmly in position while whisking in the oil, twist a damp cloth tightly around the base. This prevents it from slipping.

It is easier to add the oil gradually if it is poured from a measuring jug. This recipe makes 150 ml ($\frac{1}{4}$ pint) mayonnaise.

VARIATIONS
These variations are made by adding the ingredients to 150 ml ($\frac{1}{4}$ pint) mayonnaise.

Caper mayonnaise Add 10 ml (2 tsp) chopped capers, 5 ml (1 tsp) chopped pimento and 2.5 ml ($\frac{1}{2}$ tsp) tarragon vinegar (see page 99). Caper mayonnaise makes an ideal accompaniment for fish.

Celery mayonnaise Add 15 ml (1 tbsp) chopped celery and 15 ml (1 tbsp) snipped fresh chives.

Cucumber mayonnaise Add 30 ml (2 tbsp) finely chopped cucumber and 2.5 ml ($\frac{1}{2}$ level tsp) salt. This mayonnaise goes well with fish salads, especially crab, lobster or salmon.

Herb mayonnaise Add 30 ml (2 tbsp) snipped fresh chives and 15 ml (1 tbsp) chopped fresh parsley.

Horseradish mayonnaise Add 15 ml (1 level tbsp) horseradish sauce.

Piquant mayonnaise Add 5 ml (1 tsp) tomato ketchup, 5 ml (1 tsp) chopped stuffed olives and a pinch of paprika.

Tomato mayonnaise Add $\frac{1}{2}$ a tomato, skinned and diced, 1 spring onion, chopped, 1.25 ml ($\frac{1}{4}$ level tsp) salt and 5 ml (1 tsp) white wine vinegar or lemon juice.

Lemon mayonnaise Add the finely grated rind of 1 lemon and use lemon juice instead of vinegar.

Curry mayonnaise Add 5 ml (1 level tsp) curry powder to the egg yolk mixture before adding the oil.

Green mayonnaise Blanch 3 large spinach leaves quickly in boiling water, drain and chop finely. Add to the mayonnaise with 15 ml (1 tbsp) chopped fresh parsley and 30 ml (2 tbsp) snipped fresh chives.

Watercress mayonnaise Add $\frac{1}{4}$ of a bunch of watercress, very finely chopped to 150 ml ($\frac{1}{4}$ pint) lemon mayonnaise.

MUSTARD DRESSING

15 ml (1 level tbsp) plain flour
a pinch of cayenne pepper
25 ml (1½ level tbsp) sugar
5 ml (1 level tsp) mustard powder
2.5 ml (½ level tsp) salt
150 ml (¼ pint) milk ·
2 egg yolks, beaten
60 ml (4 tbsp) cider vinegar

Mix the dry ingredients to a smooth cream with a little of the milk. Heat the remainder of the milk and, when boiling, stir into the blended ingredients. Return the mixture to the pan and bring to the boil, stirring all the time. Cool slightly, stir in the egg yolks and again return the pan to the heat. Cook gently until the mixture thickens, but do not allow it to boil. Remove from the heat, allow to cool and stir in the vinegar.

Note Store for up to 1 week in a screw-topped jar in the refrigerator. Makes 300 ml (½ pint).

SOURED CREAM DRESSING

142-ml (5-fl oz) carton soured cream
30 ml (2 tbsp) white wine vinegar
small piece of onion, skinned and finely chopped
2.5 ml (½ level tsp) sugar
5 ml (1 level tsp) salt
freshly ground pepper

Mix all the ingredients thoroughly. Store in a screw-topped jar for up to 4 days in the refrigerator. Makes 150 ml (¼ pint).

GARLIC DRESSING

142-ml (5-fl oz) carton soured cream
30 ml (2 tbsp) cider vinegar
1 large garlic clove, skinned and crushed
salt and freshly ground pepper
a pinch of sugar

Mix all the ingredients well together. Leave to stand for several hours before use. Store for up to 4 days in a screw-topped jar in the refrigerator. Makes 150 ml (¼ pint).

PESTO

This is a traditional sauce from Italy, made from fresh basil, garlic, cheese, olive oil and sometimes pine nuts. Basil is a herb that grows very well on a sunny windowsill.

50 g (2 oz) basil leaves
2 garlic cloves, skinned
30 ml (2 level tbsp) pine nuts
salt and freshly ground pepper
50 g (2 oz) freshly grated Parmesan cheese
100 ml (4 fl oz) olive oil
30 ml (2 tbsp) double cream

Put the basil, garlic, pine nuts, salt and pepper in a mortar and grind until a paste is formed. Add the cheese and blend well. Transfer to a bowl and beat in the oil, a little at a time, stirring vigorously with a wooden spoon. When all the oil has been added, fold in the cream.

This sauce can also be made in a blender or food processor. Place the basil, garlic, pine nuts, seasoning and olive oil in the blender or food processor and blend at high speed until very creamy. Transfer the mixture to a bowl, fold in the cheese and cream and mix thoroughly. Store for up to 2 weeks in a screw-topped jar in the refrigerator or several months in a freezer. Makes about 300 ml ($\frac{1}{2}$ pint).

THOUSAND ISLAND MAYONNAISE

150 ml ($\frac{1}{4}$ pint) mayonnaise (see page 102)
15 ml (1 tbsp) chopped stuffed olives
5 ml (1 tsp) finely chopped onion
1 egg, hard-boiled, shelled and chopped
15 ml (1 tbsp) finely chopped green pepper
5 ml (1 tsp) chopped fresh parsley
5 ml (1 level tsp) tomato purée

Mix all the ingredients together until well combined. Store for up to 4 days in a screw-topped jar in the refrigerator. Makes about 200 ml (7 fl oz).

WALNUT DRESSING

If you wish to use a blender instead of a food processor to make this dressing, add a little oil with the bread mixture so that the machine will run well.

1 small slice wholemeal bread
40 g (1½ oz) walnuts
10 ml (2 tsp) lemon juice
1 garlic clove, skinned
salt and freshly ground pepper
200 ml (7 fl oz) olive oil

Remove the crusts from the slice of bread and soak it in cold water for a few minutes. Squeeze out the excess moisture and place the bread in a food processor. Add the walnuts, lemon juice, garlic and seasoning and blend at high speed until the mixture is very finely ground. Gradually add the oil through the funnel, while the machine is still running, until it is all incorporated. Check the seasoning and stir well before use. Store for up to 1 week in a screw-topped jar in the refrigerator. Makes 225 ml (8 fl oz).

PIQUANT DRESSING

1 lemon
150 ml (¼ pint) double cream
30 ml (2 tbsp) milk
125 g (4 oz) Lancashire cheese, crumbled
50 g (2 oz) full fat soft cheese
60 ml (4 tbsp) mayonnaise (see page 102)
1 spring onion, trimmed and chopped
3 parsley sprigs
2.5 ml (½ level tsp) salt
freshly ground pepper

Remove a broad strip of peel from the lemon and reserve. Using a serrated knife, cut away all the remaining peel and pith, leaving only the lemon flesh. Slice thickly, discarding the pips.

Place the lemon and the strip of peel in a blender or food processor and add all the remaining ingredients. Blend at high speed until all the ingredients are well combined. Check the seasoning and pour the dressing into a screw-topped jar to store. The dressing will keep for up to 4 days in the refrigerator. Makes about 450 ml (¾ pint).

AÏOLI

This traditional Spanish garlic dressing is very pungent but a milder version can be made, if preferred, by reducing the number of garlic cloves.

4 garlic cloves, skinned
2 egg yolks
1.25 ml ($\frac{1}{4}$ level tsp) salt
300 ml ($\frac{1}{2}$ pint) olive oil
30 ml (2 tbsp) lemon juice

Crush the garlic cloves with a little salt until a smooth paste is formed. Place in a bowl. Add the egg yolks and salt and beat well. Gradually beat in the oil, a little at a time, as for mayonnaise, until the mixture is thick and smooth. If the mixture becomes too thick, add a little of the lemon juice. When all the oil is added, beat in the remaining lemon juice. Store for up to 4 days in a screw-topped jar in the refrigerator. Makes 300 ml ($\frac{1}{2}$ pint).

GREEN GODDESS DRESSING

150 ml ($\frac{1}{4}$ pint) mayonnaise (see page 102)
142-ml (5-fl oz) carton soured cream
30 ml (2 tbsp) chopped fresh parsley
30 ml (2 tbsp) snipped fresh chives
4 anchovies, finely chopped
30 ml (2 tbsp) cider vinegar
salt and freshly ground pepper

Mix all ingredients together, seasoning well. Allow to stand for several hours before use. Store for up to 4 days in a screw-topped jar in the refrigerator. Makes about 300 ml ($\frac{1}{2}$ pint).

AVOCADO DRESSING

1 ripe avocado
15 ml (1 tbsp) lemon juice
30 ml (2 tbsp) mayonnaise (see page 102)
30 ml (2 tbsp) single cream
salt and freshly ground pepper

Halve, stone, peel and slice the avocado. Place in a blender or food processor with the remaining ingredients and blend at high speed until the dressing is velvety smooth. Check the seasoning and transfer to a screw-topped jar to store. This dressing will only keep for 1 day in the refrigerator. Makes about 300 ml ($\frac{1}{2}$ pint).

HORSERADISH DRESSING

30 ml (2 tbsp) horseradish sauce
142-ml (5-fl oz) carton soured cream, whipped
5 ml (1 level tsp) sugar
5 ml (1 tsp) lemon juice
5 ml (1 tsp) vinegar (see page 99)
salt and cayenne pepper

Mix the horseradish sauce with the cream, add the sugar, lemon juice and vinegar and season with salt and cayenne pepper to taste. Store for up to 4 days in a screw-topped jar in the refrigerator. Makes 150 ml ($\frac{1}{4}$ pint).

COOKED SALAD CREAM

45 ml (3 level tbsp) plain flour
15 ml (1 level tbsp) sugar
10 ml (2 level tsp) mustard powder
5 ml (1 level tsp) salt
150 ml ($\frac{1}{4}$ pint) milk
2 eggs, beaten
50 g (2 oz) butter
150 ml ($\frac{1}{4}$ pint) white wine vinegar
150 ml ($\frac{1}{4}$ pint) salad oil

Mix all the dry ingredients in a saucepan and blend to a smooth cream with the milk. Bring to the boil, stirring all the time, cook for 1 minute and then cool. Beat in the eggs and butter, return the pan to the heat and cook until thick, but do not allow to boil. Remove from the heat, gradually beat in the vinegar and finally stir in the oil.

This salad dressing can be used as for mayonnaise. It can also be bottled and stored for a few days in the refrigerator. Shake well before using as it tends to separate out on standing. Makes about 600 ml (1 pint).

CREAM DRESSING

150 ml ($\frac{1}{4}$ pint) double cream
salt
cayenne pepper
15–30 ml (1–2 tbsp) vinegar (see page 99)

Season the cream to taste with salt and cayenne pepper and whip until thick. Add the vinegar gradually and chill before using. Store for up to 4 days in a screw-topped jar in the refrigerator. Makes 150 ml ($\frac{1}{4}$ pint).

RÉMOULADE SAUCE

150 ml ($\frac{1}{4}$ pint) mayonnaise (see page 102)
5 ml (1 tsp) chopped gherkins
5 ml (1 tsp) chopped capers
5 ml (1 tsp) chopped fresh parsley
1 anchovy, finely chopped

Place all the ingredients in a bowl and stir together until well combined. Store for up to 4 days in a screw-topped jar in the refrigerator. Makes 150 ml ($\frac{1}{4}$ pint).

TARTARE SAUCE

150 ml ($\frac{1}{4}$ pint) mayonnaise (see page 102)
5 ml (1 tsp) chopped fresh tarragon or snipped chives
10 ml (2 tsp) chopped capers
10 ml (2 tsp) chopped gherkins
10 ml (2 tsp) chopped fresh parsley
15 ml (1 tbsp) lemon juice or tarragon vinegar (see page 99)

Mix all the ingredients well, then leave the sauce to stand for at least 1 hour before serving, to allow the flavours to blend. Serve with fish. Store for up to 4 days in a screw-topped jar in the refrigerator. Makes 150 ml ($\frac{1}{4}$ pint).

TOMATO AND YOGHURT DRESSING

60 ml (4 tbsp) olive or corn oil
5 ml (1 level tsp) salt
5 ml (1 level tsp) caster sugar
30 ml (2 tbsp) vinegar (see page 99)
300 ml ($\frac{1}{2}$ pint) tomato juice
150 ml ($\frac{1}{4}$ pint) natural yoghurt
10 ml (2 level tsp) grated onion
30 ml (2 tbsp) horseradish sauce
freshly ground pepper

Place the oil, salt, sugar, vinegar and tomato juice in a bowl and whisk well together. Gradually whisk in the yoghurt, followed by the grated onion and horseradish. Season well with pepper. Store for up to 1 week in a screw-topped jar in the refrigerator. Makes 600 ml (1 pint).

BUTTERMILK DRESSING

300 ml ($\frac{1}{2}$ pint) buttermilk
30 ml (2 tbsp) oil (see page 98)
salt and freshly ground pepper
30 ml (2 tbsp) chopped spring onions

Mix all the ingredients together. Add any of the ingredients used in variations on the French dressing recipe (page 100) to add extra flavour, if liked. Store for up to 4 days in a screw-topped jar in the refrigerator.

BLUE CHEESE DRESSING

150 ml ($\frac{1}{4}$ pint) mayonnaise (see page 102)
142-ml (5-fl oz) carton soured cream
75 g (3 oz) Blue cheese, crumbled
5 ml (1 tsp) vinegar (see page 99)
1 garlic clove, skinned and crushed
freshly ground pepper

Mix all the ingredients well together. Allow to stand for several hours before use to allow the flavours to mingle. Store for up to 1 week in a screw-topped jar in the refrigerator.

Note A slightly sharper dressing can be made using natural yoghurt instead of soured cream.

YOGHURT DRESSING

150 ml ($\frac{1}{4}$ pint) natural yoghurt
15 ml (1 tbsp) oil (see page 98)
5–10 ml (1–2 tsp) vinegar (see page 99)
5 ml (1 tsp) wholegrain mustard

Mix all the ingredients well together and chill before serving. Store for up to 1 week in a screw-topped jar in the refrigerator. Makes 150 ml ($\frac{1}{4}$ pint).

Note Yoghurt can be used as a substitute for soured cream in any recipe. It will give a slightly sharper dressing. Yoghurts vary a little in acidity—season to taste.

ACCOMPANIMENTS

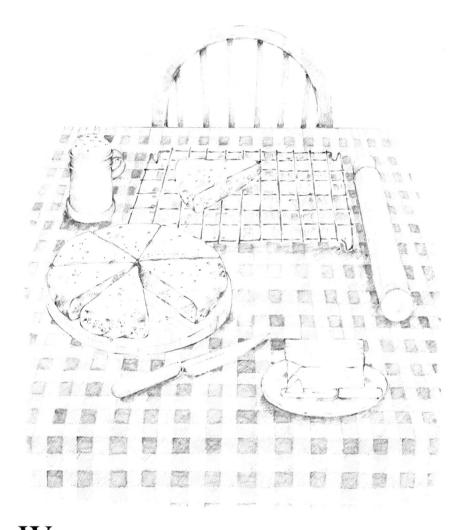

W hen serving a salad as a starter or main course, it is nice to serve something with it. This can simply be some crusty French bread or brown bread and butter, or pitta bread, but for a change, try some of the more unusual recipes for breads, rolls and biscuits in this chapter.

A delicious homemade accompaniment of Herb oatcakes (see page 118) or Walnut cheesies (see page 116) can make a salad into something special. Choose an accompanying dish that will compliment the flavours in the salad.

Some of these breads and rolls are especially nice if warmed in the oven before serving, hot and crispy, with lots of butter. They should all be served as fresh as possible and look attractive served in a basket lined with a brightly coloured paper napkin.

BAKED ANCHOVY ROLLS

Makes 8
50-g (1¾-oz) can anchovies
milk
125 g (4 oz) butter, softened
freshly ground pepper
15 ml (1 tbsp) lemon juice
3 sticks celery, trimmed and finely chopped
8 large finger rolls

Drain the anchovies from their oil, cover with a little milk and leave to soak for 20 minutes. Preheat the oven to 220°C (425°F) mark 7.

Strain off the milk and mash the anchovies with a fork until smooth. Beat in the butter with the pepper, lemon juice and celery. Make three diagonal cuts through the top of each finger roll, leaving the bottom crust intact. Spread the anchovy butter in the cuts and place the rolls side by side on a large sheet of kitchen foil. Wrap the foil loosely around them and place on a baking sheet. Bake in the centre of the oven for 15 minutes until golden. Serve piping hot.

CHEESE AND WALNUT LOAF

Serves 6
225 g (8 oz) self raising flour
2.5 ml (½ level tsp) mustard powder
a pinch of salt
50 g (2 oz) block margarine
25 g (1 oz) shelled walnuts, finely chopped
75 g (3 oz) red Leicester cheese, grated
1 egg, size 2
150 ml (¼ pint) milk

Grease and base line a 900-ml (1½-pint) loaf tin. Preheat the oven to 180°C (350°F) mark 4. Sift the flour, mustard and salt into a bowl. Cut the margarine into small pieces, add it to the bowl and rub it into the flour until the mixture resembles fine breadcrumbs. Stir in the walnuts and cheese. Beat the egg and milk together and use to bind the mixture to a very soft dough.

Spoon the mixture into the prepared loaf tin and bake in the centre of the oven for about 45 minutes until golden brown. Turn out and leave to cool on a wire rack.

POPPY SEED KNOTS

Makes 8
283-g (10-oz) packet white bread mix
200 ml (7 fl oz) lukewarm milk
beaten egg
poppy seeds

Thoroughly grease a baking sheet. Make up and knead the dough according to packet instructions, using milk instead of water. Divide the dough into eight, roll each piece into a long sausage shape and tie loosely in a single knot. Place well apart on the prepared baking sheet, cover loosely with a clean, damp tea towel, set aside in a warm place and leave to rise for about 40 minutes until doubled in size. Towards the end of the rising time, preheat the oven to 230°C (450°F) mark 8.

Uncover the rolls and brush evenly with beaten egg to which a pinch of salt has been added. Sprinkle with poppy seeds and bake in the centre of the oven for about 12 minutes until risen and golden brown. Transfer the knots to a wire rack and leave to cool.

CHEESE LOAF

450 g (1 lb) strong plain white flour
10 ml (2 level tsp) salt
5 ml (1 level tsp) mustard powder
freshly ground pepper
100–175 g (4–6 oz) Cheddar cheese, grated
15 g ($\frac{1}{2}$ oz) fresh yeast or 30 ml (2 level tbsp) dried yeast and 2.5 ml ($\frac{1}{2}$ level tsp) sugar
300 ml ($\frac{1}{2}$ pint) tepid water

Grease two 450-g (1-lb) loaf tins. Sift the flour, salt, mustard and pepper into a large bowl. Stir in three quarters of the cheese. Blend the fresh yeast and water together. If using dried yeast, dissolve the sugar in the water, sprinkle the yeast over and leave for 10–15 minutes until frothy.

Add the yeast liquid to the dry ingredients and mix to a soft dough. Turn on to a lightly floured surface and knead for 10 minutes. Cover with a clean, damp tea towel and leave to rise in a warm place for about 45 minutes until doubled in size.

Uncover the dough, turn on to a floured surface and knead for 5 minutes. Divide the dough into two and shape to fit the tins. Cover with a clean, damp tea towel and leave to prove in a warm place for about 20 minutes until the dough reaches the tops of the tins. Towards the end of the proving time, preheat the oven to 190°C (375°F) mark 5.

Uncover the tins, sprinkle the tops of the loaves with the remaining cheese and bake in the centre of the oven for 40–45 minutes until well risen and golden brown. Turn the loaves out on to a wire rack and leave to cool. Makes two 450-g (1-lb) loaves.

HOT HERB BREAD

Illustrated in colour facing page 33

Serves 4
100 g (4 oz) butter, softened
60 ml (4 tbsp) chopped fresh parsley
salt and freshly ground pepper
1 small French loaf (about 30.5 cm/12 inches long)

Individual crusty rolls can be treated in the same way. Preheat the oven to 180°C (350°F) mark 4. Cream the butter, parsley and seasonings well together. Cut the bread into diagonal slices about 2.5 cm (1 inch) thick and sandwich the loaf together again with the herb butter. Wrap the loaf in kitchen foil, place on a baking sheet and bake in the oven for about 20 minutes. Serve piping hot.

VARIATION
Garlic bread Follow the recipe above but omit the herbs and add 1 garlic clove, skinned and crushed, to the butter.

BROWN BREAD STICKS

Illustrated in colour facing page 32

Makes 24
283-g (10-oz) packet brown bread mix
beaten egg
caraway or celery seeds

Make up and knead the dough according to packet instructions. Divide the dough into 24 pieces and roll each one to a thin sausage shape about 15 cm (6 inches) long. Place them side by side, not too close together, on a baking sheet. Cover loosely with a clean, damp tea towel, set aside in a warm place and leave to rise for about 40 minutes until doubled in size. Towards the end of the rising time, preheat the oven to 220°C (425°F) mark 7.

Uncover the bread sticks, brush with beaten egg and sprinkle with caraway or celery seeds. Bake in the centre of the oven for 12–15 minutes until risen and golden brown. Transfer to a wire rack and leave to cool.

MELBA TOAST

Illustrated in colour facing page 48

Toast 0.5-cm ($\frac{1}{4}$-inch) slices of bread. Split them horizontally and toast the uncooked surfaces. Ready-cut thin-sliced bread is ideal.

Alternatively, cut stale bread into very thin slices, lay them on baking sheets and dry off in the bottom of a very low oven, until they are crisp and curled slightly. Before serving, brown them off slightly under a very low grill.

SAVOURY CURLS

Makes 15
50 g (2 oz) plain flour
a pinch of salt
5 ml (1 level tsp) paprika
50 g (2 oz) butter
50 g (2 oz) full fat soft cheese, chilled
yeast extract

Sift the flour, salt and paprika into a bowl. Cut the butter into small pieces, add it to the bowl and rub it into the flour until the mixture resembles fine breadcrumbs. Add the cheese and work it into the mixture to form a soft dough. Knead lightly on a floured surface, then wrap in cling film and chill.

Thoroughly grease a baking sheet. Preheat the oven to 200°C (400°F) mark 6. Place the dough on a lightly floured surface and roll out to an oblong measuring about 35 × 10 cm (15 × 4 inches). Spread very thinly with yeast extract and roll up lengthways to make a Swiss roll shape. Cut the roll into 15 pieces 2.5 cm (1 inch) long. Make two cuts across the top of each piece, going three quarters of the way across. Fan out the three little slices and flatten them so that the circles of yeast extract are exposed. Place on the prepared baking sheet and bake in the oven for about 10 minutes until golden. Transfer the curls to a wire rack and leave to cool.

BUTTER THINS

Makes about 20
225 g (8 oz) plain flour
2.5 ml ($\frac{1}{2}$ level tsp) salt
5 ml (1 level tsp) baking powder
50 g (2 oz) butter or block margarine
75–90 ml (5–6 tbsp) water
beaten egg
rock salt

Thoroughly grease a baking sheet. Preheat the oven to 180°C (350°F) mark 4. Sift the flour, salt and baking powder into a bowl. Cut the fat into small pieces, add it to the bowl and rub it into the flour until the mixture resembles fine breadcrumbs. Bind to a soft but manageable dough with the water. Roll out very thinly on a lightly floured surface and stamp out 7.5-cm (3-inch) plain rounds. Place on the prepared baking sheet, prick well with a fork, brush with beaten egg and sprinkle with rock salt. Bake in the oven for 15–20 minutes until golden. Transfer to a wire rack and leave to cool.

WALNUT CHEESIES

Makes 9
283-g (10-oz) packet brown bread mix
125 g (4 oz) full fat soft cheese
15–30 ml (1–2 tbsp) single cream
25 g (1 oz) shelled walnuts, finely chopped
salt and freshly ground pepper

Grease and base line a 16-cm (6½-inch) square cake tin. Make up and knead the dough according to packet instructions. Roll out on a lightly floured surface to a 30.5-cm (12-inch) square.

Beat the cheese with the cream, walnuts and seasoning and spread over the dough. Roll up and cut into nine even-sized pieces. Place cut-side down in the prepared cake tin. Cover loosely with a clean, damp tea towel, set aside in a warm place and leave to rise for about 40 minutes until doubled in size. Towards the end of the rising time, preheat the oven to 230°C (450°F) mark 8.

Uncover the cheesies and bake in the centre of the oven for about 20 minutes until risen and golden brown. Turn the cheesies out of the tin on to a wire rack and leave to cool.

PARKERHOUSE ROLLS

Makes 8
283-g (10-oz) packet white bread mix
30 ml (2 tbsp) finely chopped fresh thyme
200 ml (7 fl oz) water, hand hot
melted butter to glaze

Mix together the dry bread mix and chopped thyme and stir in the water. Draw the dough together in the bowl, turn on to a lightly floured surface and knead for about 5 minutes. Roll the dough out to 1 cm (½ inch) thickness. Using a 6.5-cm (2½-inch) plain cutter, press out eight rounds, re-rolling the dough as necessary. With the blunt edge of a knife, make a crease just off centre of each round. Brush each round with melted butter and fold over so the larger part overlaps. Press well together. Place on a baking sheet, cover loosely with a clean, damp tea towel, set aside in a warm place and leave to rise for about 40 minutes, until doubled in size. Towards the end of the rising time, preheat the oven to 230°C (450°F) mark 8.

Uncover the rolls, brush again with melted butter and bake in the centre of the oven for 10–12 minutes until risen and golden brown. Transfer from the baking sheet to a wire rack and leave to cool. Serve soon after baking, while still very fresh.

BUTTER WHIRLS

Makes 12
283-g (10-oz) packet white bread mix
50 g (2 oz) butter, softened
15 ml (1 level tbsp) coarse-grain mustard
salt and freshly ground pepper

Thoroughly grease a baking sheet. Make up and knead the dough according to the packet instructions. Roll out on a lightly floured surface to a 30.5-cm (12-inch) square.

Beat the butter, mustard and seasoning together and spread over the dough. Roll up the dough, place on the prepared baking sheet and join the ends together to form a ring. Slash the dough at 2.5-cm (1-inch) intervals to within 1 cm ($\frac{1}{2}$ inch) of the centre edge. Cover loosely with a clean, damp tea towel, set aside in a warm place and leave to rise for about 40 minutes until doubled in size. Towards the end of the rising time, preheat the oven to 230°C (450°F) mark 8.

Uncover the ring and bake in the oven for about 15 minutes until risen and golden brown. Transfer the ring to a wire rack and leave to cool. Break the ring into twelve whirls before serving.

HOT MUSTARD FINGER ROLLS

Makes 8
8 wholemeal finger rolls
75 g (3 oz) butter, softened
10 ml (2 level tsp) French mustard

Preheat the oven to 200°C (400°F) mark 6. Cut the finger rolls almost through to the base at 2.5-cm (1-inch) intervals. Beat together the butter and mustard and spread on the cut surfaces of the rolls. Place on a baking sheet and bake in the oven for 10–15 minutes until hot.

CROÛTONS

day old bread
vegetable oil
salt, garlic salt or curry powder (optional)

Remove the crusts from the bread and cut into 0.5–1-cm ($\frac{1}{4}$–$\frac{1}{2}$-inch) cubes. Heat the oil in a frying pan and fry the bread cubes until golden and crisp, stirring frequently. Drain the croûtons on absorbent kitchen paper and sprinkle with salt, garlic salt or curry powder, if liked.

FLAKY PÂTÉ PUFFS

Makes 20
125 g (4 oz) soft liver pâté
15 ml (1 level tbsp) Dijon mustard
50 g (2 oz) salted mixed nuts, finely chopped
freshly ground black pepper
368-g (13-oz) packet frozen puff pastry, thawed
beaten egg

Preheat the oven to 220°C (425°F) mark 7. Place the pâté, mustard, half the nuts and the pepper in a bowl and beat well together. Roll out the pastry thinly on a lightly floured surface and stamp out about 20 rounds using a 9-cm (3½-inch) plain cutter. Gather together and reroll the trimmings as necessary.

Place a small spoonful of pâté mixture in the centre of each round and brush the edges of the pastry with beaten egg. Fold over the pastry to form half-moon shapes and seal the edges well together. Place the puffs on ungreased baking sheets, brush with beaten egg and sprinkle with the remaining nuts. Bake in the oven for 12–15 minutes until risen and golden brown. Transfer to a wire rack and leave to cool.

HERB OATCAKES

Makes 8
25 g (1 oz) lard
75 ml (3 fl oz) water
225 g (8 oz) medium oatmeal
2.5 ml (½ level tsp) dried sage
1.25 ml (¼ level tsp) bicarbonate of soda
1.25 ml (¼ level tsp) salt

Preheat the oven to 180°C (350°F) mark 4. Place the lard and water in a small saucepan and heat until the lard has melted, then leave to cool. Mix together the oatmeal, sage, bicarbonate of soda and salt. Stir in the cool liquid, using a palette knife and mix to a moist dough, adding a little more water if necessary.

Turn the dough on to an ungreased baking sheet and, using one flour-covered hand, pat it out to a 20.5-cm (8-inch) round. Roll lightly over the surface to flatten, and neaten the edges. Bake in the oven for about 40 minutes until golden. Cut into eight wedges while still warm and allow to firm up slightly before transferring to a wire rack to cool.

WHOLEMEAL BISCUITS

Makes 12
175 g (6 oz) plain wholemeal flour
120 ml (8 level tbsp) bran
a good pinch of salt
15 g ($\frac{1}{2}$ oz) sesame seeds
75 g (3 oz) butter
1 egg, size 2, beaten

Preheat the oven to 190°C (375°F) mark 5. Combine the flour, bran, salt and sesame seeds in a bowl. Cut the butter into small pieces, add it to the flour and rub it in until the mixture resembles fine breadcrumbs. Bind the mixture with the egg and 15–30 ml (1–2 tbsp) water. Roll out on a lightly floured surface and stamp out twelve rounds using a 7.5-cm (3-inch) plain cutter. Place on ungreased baking sheets and bake in the oven for about 15 minutes until brown. Allow to cool slightly on the baking sheets, then transfer to wire racks and leave to cool completely.

VARIATIONS
1. Add 50 g (2 oz) Cheddar cheese, grated and 15 ml (1 tbsp) dried onion flakes before adding the egg.
2. Add 1 garlic clove, skinned and crushed, before adding the egg.

CHEESE STRAWS

Makes 24
75 g (3 oz) plain flour
salt and freshly ground pepper
40 g ($1\frac{1}{2}$ oz) butter
40 g ($1\frac{1}{2}$ oz) Cheddar cheese, use Blue cheese as a variation, if liked
1 egg, beaten
5 ml (1 level tsp) French mustard
grated Parmesan cheese

Preheat the oven to 180°C (350°F) mark 4. Mix the flour and seasonings together in a bowl. Cut the butter into small pieces, add it to the flour and rub it in until the mixture resembles fine breadcrumbs. Grate in the cheese straight from the refrigerator. Stir to mix evenly.

Combine half the beaten egg with the French mustard and stir it into the flour mixture to form a soft dough. Turn on to a lightly floured surface and knead a little until just smooth. Roll out the dough to a 15-cm (6-inch) square and place on a baking sheet. Brush with the remaining beaten egg and sprinkle with Parmesan cheese. Divide the dough into straws 7.5 cm (3 inches) long and 1 cm ($\frac{1}{2}$ inch) wide and separate. Bake in the oven for 12–15 minutes until golden. Transfer to a wire rack and leave to cool. Store in an airtight container until required.

BRAN MUFFINS

Makes about 16
50 g (2 oz) bran
250 ml (8 fl oz) milk
25 g (1 oz) butter, softened
30 ml (2 level tbsp) caster sugar
1 egg, beaten
125 g (4 oz) plain flour
2.5 ml ($\frac{1}{2}$ level tsp) salt
15 ml (3 level tsp) baking powder

Thoroughly grease sixteen deep 6.5-cm ($2\frac{1}{2}$-inch) diameter patty tins. Preheat the oven to 190°C (375°F) mark 5. Soak the bran in the milk for 5 minutes.

Meanwhile, beat the butter until creamy and gradually beat in the sugar. Add the egg, a little at a time, beating well after each addition, then stir in the bran and milk mixture.

Sift the flour, salt and baking powder together and stir lightly into the creamed ingredients until just mixed. Spoon into the patty tins to two thirds full. Bake in the oven for about 25 minutes, or until golden brown and firm to the touch. Ease out of the tins, transfer to a wire rack and leave to cool. Split and butter to serve.

WHOLEMEAL SCONE FINGERS

To lighten the texture of the scones, use half plain white and half plain wholemeal flour.

Makes 6
225 g (8 oz) plain wholemeal flour
15 ml (3 level tsp) baking powder
1.25 ml ($\frac{1}{4}$ level tsp) ground coriander
1.25 ml ($\frac{1}{4}$ level tsp) paprika
salt and freshly ground pepper
50 g (2 oz) butter
75 g (3 oz) Cheddar cheese, grated
about 150 ml ($\frac{1}{4}$ pint) milk

Thoroughly grease a baking sheet. Preheat the oven to 230°C (450°F) mark 8. Place the flour, baking powder, spices and seasoning in a large bowl and mix well together. Cut the butter into small pieces, add it to the flour and rub it in until the mixture resembles fine breadcrumbs. Stir in the cheese, reserving 45 ml (3 tbsp), and bind the mixture to a soft dough with the milk. Knead lightly, turn on to the prepared baking sheet and pat the dough out to an oblong measuring about 20.5 × 12.5 cm (8 × 5 inches). Neaten the edges and scatter over the reserved cheese. Bake in the oven for 12–15 minutes, or until well browned and firm to the touch. Allow to cool slightly before cutting into fingers. Serve warm with butter.

CHEESE AND BACON SHORTIES

Makes about 20	
125 g (4 oz) streaky bacon, rinded	
175 g (6 oz) plain flour	
2.5 ml ($\frac{1}{2}$ level tsp) mustard powder	
1.25 ml ($\frac{1}{4}$ level tsp) paprika	
salt and freshly ground pepper	
125 g (4 oz) butter	
125 g (4 oz) Cheddar cheese, grated	

Preheat the oven to 180°C (350°F) mark 4. Grill the bacon until crisp, cool and snip into small pieces. Sift the flour, mustard, paprika and seasoning into a bowl. Cut the butter into small pieces, add it to the flour and rub it in until the mixture resembles fine breadcrumbs. Stir in the bacon and grated cheese and work the mixture together to form a soft dough.

Press the mixture into an oblong tin measuring 28×18 cm (11×7 inches). Level the surface and bake in the oven for about 35 minutes until golden. Allow to cool slightly, then cut into fingers and ease out of the tin. Leave to cool completely on a wire rack.

CHEESE BITES

Makes about 70
100 g (4 oz) butter
100 g (4 oz) plain flour
100 g (4 oz) Cheddar cheese, grated
salt and freshly ground pepper
a pinch of paprika
beaten egg

Preheat the oven to 200°C (400°F) mark 6. Cut the butter into small pieces and rub it into the flour until the mixture resembles fine breadcrumbs. Add the cheese and seasoning. Gather together using the fingertips of one hand and knead to a smooth paste.

Roll out on a lightly floured surface to about 0.5 cm ($\frac{1}{4}$ inch) thickness. Using a 4-cm ($1\frac{1}{2}$-inch) plain round cutter, stamp out as many rounds as possible. Gather the trimmings together, reroll and continue until all the dough is used. Alternatively, cut into similar-sized triangles. Arrange on baking sheets and brush lightly with beaten egg. Bake in the oven for about 10 minutes until golden. Allow to cool slightly on the baking sheets before transferring to wire racks to cool completely.

CHEESE AND CHIVE HOTTIES

1 medium fresh uncut white sandwich loaf
butter or margarine, softened
225 g (8 oz) red Leicester cheese, grated
snipped fresh chives
salt and freshly ground pepper
melted butter
paprika

Chill the loaf in the freezer or the freezing compartment of the refrigerator for 30 minutes to make slicing easier. Cut as many thin slices as possible along the whole length of the loaf and spread with butter or margarine. Remove the crusts.

Sprinkle each slice with cheese, chives and seasoning. Roll each slice up from the shorter edge and wrap in dampened greaseproof paper. Return to the freezer and chill for 30 minutes more.

Preheat the oven to 230°C (450°F) mark 8. Unwrap the rolls, arrange them on baking sheets, brush with melted butter and dust with paprika. Bake in the oven for 5–10 minutes until golden. Transfer to a wire rack and leave to cool.

CHEESE PALMIERS

Makes 10
212-g (7½-oz) packet puff pastry, thawed
beaten egg
75 g (3 oz) Gruyere cheese, grated
salt and freshly ground pepper
paprika

Roll out the pastry to an oblong 30.5 × 25.5 cm (12 × 10 inch) and brush it with beaten egg. Scatter the grated cheese over the pastry and sprinkle it with salt, pepper and paprika.

Roll the pastry up tightly lengthwise, rolling from each side until the rolls meet in the centre. Cut it across into ten pieces. Place the pieces cut side down on a greased baking sheet and flatten them with the heel of the hand.

Bake in the oven at 200°C (400°F) mark 6 for 15–18 minutes, or until brown and crisp. Ease the palmiers off the baking sheet and cool them on a wire rack.

CHEESE D'ARTOIS

Makes 20–24
1 egg, beaten
25 g (1 oz) butter, melted
50 g (2 oz) Cheddar cheese, grated
salt and freshly ground pepper
212-g (7½-oz) packet frozen puff pastry, thawed
beaten egg to glaze

Mix the beaten egg, butter and cheese to a smooth cream and season well. Roll out the pastry thinly to a 33-cm (13-inch) square, cut in half and place one half on a baking sheet. Spread the cheese mixture over the pastry to within 0.5 cm (¼ inch) of the edges. Dampen the edges with water and cover with the remaining pastry. Brush with the beaten egg to glaze and mark the pastry into fingers. Bake in the oven at 200°C (400°F) mark 6 for about 10–15 minutes until well risen and golden brown. Cut into fingers before serving.

QUICK WHOLEMEAL BREAD

Makes 2 loaves
15 g (½ oz) fresh yeast or 10 ml (2 level tsp)
dried yeast and 5 ml (1 level tsp) caster sugar
about 300 ml (½ pint) tepid water
5 ml (1 level tsp) sugar
450 g (1 lb) plain wholemeal flour or 225 g
(8 oz) plain wholemeal and 225 g (8 oz) strong
plain flour
5–10 ml (1–2 level tsp) salt
25 g (1 oz) lard

Blend the fresh yeast with the water. If using dried yeast, dissolve the sugar in 150 ml (¼ pint) water, sprinkle the yeast over and leave for about 20 minutes until frothy. Grease a baking sheet.

Mix the sugar, flour and salt together in a large bowl and rub in the fat. Make a well in the centre, add the yeast liquid, and remaining water if using dried yeast, and mix with a wooden spoon to give a fairly soft dough, adding more water if necessary.

Turn the dough on to a lightly floured surface and knead well until smooth. Divide the dough into two, shape into rounds and put on the baking sheet. Cover with a clean damp cloth and leave to rise in a warm place for about 1 hour until the rounds have nearly doubled in size.

Bake the loaves in the oven at 230°C (450°F) mark 8 for about 15 minutes, reduce the heat to 200°C (450°F) mark 6 and bake for a further 20–30 minutes.

QUICK WHITE LOAF

Makes two 450-g (1-lb) loaves
15 g ($\frac{1}{2}$ oz) fresh yeast or 7.5 ml (1$\frac{1}{2}$ level tsp)
dried yeast and 5 ml (1 level tsp) caster sugar
about 300 ml ($\frac{1}{2}$ pint) tepid water
450 g (1 lb) strong plain flour
5 ml (1 level tsp) salt
cracked wheat

Grease two 450-g (1-lb) loaf tins. Blend the fresh yeast with the water. If using dried yeast, dissolve the sugar in the water, sprinkle the yeast over and leave for about 20 minutes until frothy.

Mix the flour and salt together in a large bowl, make a well in the centre and add the yeast liquid. Mix to an elastic dough, adding more water if necessary. Turn on to a lightly floured surface and knead for 5–10 minutes until the dough is really smooth.

Divide the dough into two portions and put into the prepared tins. Brush the tops with water and sprinkle with cracked wheat. Cover the tins with a clean damp cloth and leave to rise in a warm place for about 1 hour until the dough comes to the tops of the tins.

Bake the loaves in the oven at 230°C (450°F) mark 8 for 30–40 minutes until well risen and golden brown. When the loaves are cooked they will shrink slightly from the sides of the tins and will sound hollow when tapped on the bottom.

WHOLEMEAL ROUND

50 g (2 oz) plain flour
a pinch of salt
15 ml (1 level tbsp) baking powder
175 g (6 oz) plain wholemeal flour
50 g (2 oz) caster sugar
50 g (2 oz) butter or block margarine
about 150 ml ($\frac{1}{4}$ pint) milk

Sift together the plain flour, salt and baking powder into a bowl. Add the wholemeal flour and sugar. Lightly rub in the fat and mix to a soft but manageable dough with milk.

Turn the dough on to a lightly floured surface and shape into a flat 15-cm (6-inch) round. Place on a preheated ungreased baking sheet and mark into six triangles with the back of a floured knife. Bake in the oven at once at 220°C (425°F) mark 7 for about 15 minutes until firm and brown. Serve warm, split and buttered.

Note If using self raising wholemeal flour, reduce the baking powder quantity to 5 ml (1 level tsp).

INDEX